CW0742325

Shakespeare's Christmas

Shakespeare's Christmas

THE FESTIVE SEASON IN EARLY MODERN ENGLAND

The
History
Press

First published 1996
This revised and updated edition first published 2024

The History Press
97 St George's Place, Cheltenham,
Gloucestershire, GL50 3QB
www.thehistorypress.co.uk

British Library Cataloguing in Publication Data.
A catalogue record for this book is available from the British Library.

ISBN 978 1 80399 762 9

Typesetting and origination by The History Press
Printed and bound in Great Britain by TJ Books Limited, Padstow, Cornwall.

Proudly supporting

Trees for LYfe

Contents

Introduction

ANDREW HUBERT VON STAUFER

There has always been a great deal of debate about the authorship of Shakespeare's works, which is well beyond the scope of this revision to *Shakespeare's Christmas* – originally researched by my late wife Maria and me, and first published some three decades ago.

There is a relevance to questions about William Shakespeare that we were busy exploring at the time when the manuscript was submitted – namely about his religion. He was born at a time when religious identity could be confusing and dangerous. There have since been a number of questions raised –most notably by the former Anglican Archbishop of Canterbury Rowan Willams –as to whether the Shakespeare family were in fact recusant Catholics.

Any such leanings would certainly have coloured William's attitude to Christmas, but the reasons are both historically and politically confusing to our twenty-first-century lay perspective.

Mary Tudor, who was a half sister to Elizabeth I, had tried to reaffirm the practice and hierarchy of the Roman Catholic faith, following the rather lax and fractured break with Rome, mostly for financial and political reasons, occasioned by her father Henry VIII in the 1530s. Mary's reign ended in 1558 and as the first surviving child of Henry was, in many respects, popular.

By the time that William Shakespeare was born in 1564, many of those with land and royal favours granted by Mary had been very cautious about not upsetting the new regime under Elizabeth, who was in most respects a Protestant. Basically, most people tried to avoid controversy by effectively obeying the last order while keeping their options open. Lifespans were short then and nobody could be sure that the official religion of England would not change, should an unmarried Elizabeth die young.

This in many ways affected the celebration of Christmas throughout the following five decades of William Shakespeare's life.

The sixteenth century was a time of great artistic movement in Europe with the emergence of much symbolism, which would be developed into what we would recognise today.

The nativity scene had become a major expression of art both in painting and what we now know as the Christmas Crib, particularly, but not exclusively, in Italy and Provence. There had been a brief flowering of sculptured nativity art with the Nottingham School of Alablasters [*sic*], but that had not really caught on, as some of the more puritanically minded contemporary churchmen, who had favoured translation of the bible into English, wanted litany in the vernacular and a greater emphasis on scriptural authenticity away from the sacramental – what they called graven images and anything that smacked of relict popery and paganism. The last two were often bundled together in the haranguing sermons of Latimer & Cranmer in England and, later, John Knox in Scotland.

Throughout southern Europe – many parts of Germany and Poland in particular – the Counter Reformation was going firmly in the other direction with a formalisation of liturgy; the emergence of midnight Mass as we would recognise it; the popularisation of the nativity scene; and an encouragement of Marian devotion, with many stories about the Virgin Mary, the birth in the stable and Star of Bethlehem, the Magi and, surprisingly, the Christmas Tree in the German-speaking lands as a symbol of light, hope and legends about its shape being a reminder of the Holy Trinity.

This rather left England behind, as the surviving celebration was an adaptation of what went before with far less imagery, a greater use of greenery (bay, yew and rosemary being popular additions to the still well known holly and ivy.)

Food and drink were the great survivors, less likely to cause controversy or any hint of allegiance to Rome, especially since *Regnans in Excelsis* (Reigning on High), a papal bull excommunicating Elizabeth, was promulgated by Pope Pius V on 25 February 1570, six years after William's birth.

Unfortunately, having formalised an English Protestant religion, Elizabeth had effectively let the cat out of the bag as a number of radical Christians were drifting towards a disapproval of all celebration that could be interpreted as either Papist or Pagan, to such an extent that within thirty years of William's death, Christmas was effectively banned by Parliament!

So, it is against this confused background of secular and religious celebration, where even not appearing in an Anglican church could result in a fine, you may read on about Christmas in the time of William Shakespeare.

Andrew Hubert von Staufer
February 2024

The Christmas Entertainments

WILLIAM FRANCIS DAWSON

Shakespeare was certainly born at a fortuitous time to succeed as a playwright. Queen Elizabeth I adored the play, and under her roof it grew to the height of importance. She kept singing boys, actors and musicians, and formed several companies of players and theatrical performers. Shakespeare was commanded to write new plays for her court regularly, and she probably enjoyed the presence of this dashing and flamboyant character. The following description of the Queen's household players, and her contribution to theatrical entertainment, includes a charming anecdote about Shakespeare himself, and is from Dawson's Christmas and its Associations (1903).

The Christmas entertainments of Queen Elizabeth were enlivened by the beautiful singing of the children of her Majesty's Chapel. Queen Elizabeth I retained on her Royal establishment four sets of singing boys; which belonged to the Cathedral of St. Paul's; the Abbey of Westminster; St. George's Chapel Windsor and the Household Chapel. For the support and reinforcement of her musical bands, Elizabeth, like the other English Sovereigns, issued warrants for taking 'up suche apt and meete children, as are fitt to be instructed and framed in the Art and Science of Musicke and Singing.'

The children of the Chapel were also employed in the theatrical exhibitions represented at Court, for which their musical education had peculiarly qualified them. Richard Edwards, an eminent poet and musician of the 16th century, had written two comedies; 'Damon & Pythias' and 'Palemon & Arcite', which according to Wood, were often acted before the Queen, both at Court and at Oxford. With the latter of these the Queen was so delighted she promised Edwards a reward, which she subsequently gave him by making him first Gentleman of her Chapel, and in 1561 Master of the Children upon the death of Richard Bowyer.

As the Queen was particularly attached to dramatic entertainments, about 1569, she formed the children of the Royal Chapel into a company of theatrical performers, and placed them under the superintendence of Edwards. Not long after she formed a second society of players under the title, 'Children of the Revells' and by these two companies all Lyly's plays, and many of Shakespeare's and Jonson's were first performed. Ben Jonson has celebrated one of the chapel children, named Salathiel Pavy, who was famous for his performance of old men, but who died about 1601 aged thirteen.

The Shakespearean period had its grand Christmases, for The Christmas Players at the Court of Queen Elizabeth included England's greatest dramatist, William Shakespeare; and the Queen not only took delight in witnessing Shakespeare's plays, but also admired the poet as a player. The histrionic ability of Shakespeare was by no means contemptible, though probably not such as to have transmitted his name to posterity had he confined himself exclusively to acting. Rowe informs us that, 'the tip-top of his performances was the ghost in his own Hamlet', Aubrey states that, 'He doth act exceedingly well' and Cheetle, a contemporary of the poet, who had seem him perform, assures us that, 'he was excellent in the quality that he professed.'

An anecdote is preserved in connection with Shakespeare's playing before Queen Elizabeth I. While he was taking the part of a king, Elizabeth rose, and, in crossing the stage, dropped her glove as she passed the poet. No notice was taken by him of the incident; and the queen, desirous of finding out whether this was the result of inadvertence, or a determination to preserve the consistency of his part, moved again towards him, and again dropped her glove. Shakespeare then stooped down to pick it up, saying, in the character of the monarch whom he was playing 'And though now bent on this high embassy/ Yet stoop we to take up our cousin's glove.'

He then retired and presented the glove to the Queen, who was highly pleased with his courtly performance.

Tribute
by Digression

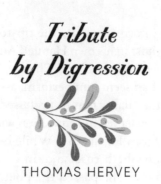

THOMAS HERVEY

Shakespeare knew how to appeal to the tastes of the great Queen Elizabeth I, a skill noted, but possibly misinterpreted, by the historian of popular antiquities, Thomas Hervey, writing in the late eighteenth and early nineteenth centuries. Hervey specialized in Christmas, and was one of the great scholars who researched and recorded the ancient customs before they died away in the later Georgian reigns. His history of Christmas was, and possibly still is, second to none, but in the course of discussing the festivities of an Elizabethan Christmas, he is desperately sidetracked in his total adulation of the great Bard! The points he makes are most valid, the manner in which he writes is cringingly comical at times. (The following text is adapted and abridged from the original which is too flowery and opinionated for our purposes, but readers may find it in Hervey's **Booke of Christmasse** [1833].)

Our readers, we think, need scarcely be told that the successor to this stern and miserable queen (Queen Mary) was sure to seize upon the old pageantries. . . . From all the old altars which the court had reared to old Father Christmas of yore, a cloud of incense was poured into the royal closet enough to choke anything but the Tudor queen. The festival was saved, and even embellished; but the saint, as far as the court was concerned, was changed. However, the example of the festivity to the people was the same; and the land was a merry land, and the Christmas time a merry time, throughout its length and breadth in the time of Queen Elizabeth.

Under these impulses, the old dramatic entertainments took a higher character and assumed a more consistent form. The first regular English tragedy, called 'Ferrex and Porrex' and the entertainment of 'Gammer Gurton's Needle' were both productions of the early period of the Queen's reign:— and amid the crowd of her worshippers rose up – with the star upon his forehead which will burn there for all time, – the very first of all created beings, William Shakespeare. These are among the strange anomalies which the world, as it is constituted, so often presents; and must present at times, constitute it how we will. – Shakespeare doing homage to Queen Elizabeth I! – The loftiest genius and the noblest heart that have yet walked this earth, in a character merely human, bowing down before this woman, with the soul of a milliner, and no heart at all! – The swayer of hearts, the ruler of men's minds, in virtue of his own transcendent nature, recognising the supremacy of this overgrown child, because she presided over the temporalities of a half emancipated nation.

To any who will amuse himself by looking over the miracle plays and masques which were replaced by the more regular forms of dramatic entertainment, and will then regale himself by the perusal of the two plays already mentioned, which came forward with higher pretentions in the beginning of this reign, there will appear reason to be sufficiently astonished at the rapid strides by which dramatic excellence was attained before its close, and during the next reign, even without taking Shakespeare into account at all.

But when we turn to the marvels of this great magician, and find that, in his hands, not only were the forms of the drama perfected, but that, – without impeding the action or interest invested in those forms, and despite his excursions into the regions of imagination and his creations out of the natural world, – he has touched every branch of human knowledge and struck into every train of human thought, that, without learning, in the popular sense, he has arrived at all the results, and embodied all the wisdom, which learning is only useful if it teaches. We can be placed in no imaginable circumstances, and under the influence of no possible feelings, of which we do not find exponents on his page, and above all, when we find that all the final morals to be drawn from his writings are hopeful ones, – that all the lessons which are his agents – joy or sorrow, pain or pleasure, are made alike to teach, are lessons of goodness, and it is impossible to attribute all this to aught but a revelation, or ascribe to him any character but that of a prophet.

Shakespeare knew more than any other mere man ever knew; and none can tell how that knowledge came to him. 'All men's business and bosoms' lay open to him. We should not like to have him quoted against us on any subject. Nothing escaped him, and he never made a mistake (we are not speaking of technical ones). He was the universal interpreter into any language of the human mind; and he knew all the myriad voices by which nature speaks. He reminds us of the Vizier in the Eastern story, who is said to understand the language of all animals. The uttering of the elements, the voices of the beasts and of birds, Shakespeare could translate into the language of men; and the thoughts and sentiments of men he rendered into words as sweet as the singing of birds.

But we are digressing – and who does not, when the image of Shakespeare comes across him?!

Elizabethan Christmas

MICHAEL HARRISON

Through her love of theatrical entertainment, Queen Elizabeth I gave patronage and credence to the stage in the late sixteenth and early seventeenth centuries. It might be said that thanks to her William Shakespeare, and the many who followed his example, are so well known today. She acceded to the throne of England just seven years before Shakespeare was born and so he grew up in an England both tolerant and favourable towards those with theatrical leanings. Drama had become fashionable. No longer the entertainment of the street, plays and pageants were now elevated to the Royal Court and noble houses.

Michael Harrison wrote extensively on traditional and historical customs in the 1950s. The following extract is from the **Tatler** magazine in 1951, which aptly describes a Christmas at the Court of Queen Elizabeth, with a particular emphasis on the evolution of theatrical entertainment and the stage under Elizabeth's patronage, from which Shakespeare would have benefited, having spent many Christmases at Queen Elizabeth's court producing plays for her.

O n November 17th (old style) Elizabeth succeeded to the throne on the death of her elder sister Mary, and Elizabeth's first Christmas as Queen was spent in making preparations for the Coronation, which had been fixed for January 15th following.

Elizabeth's differences with her sister are too well known not to mention here; it is necessary only to state that those differences did not include any difference on the subject of the respect which ought to be paid to Christmas except that Elizabeth's were gayer, more magnificent and generally much more costly than those of Mary's reign.

Elizabeth inherited all her father's liking for boisterous pleasures, as witness this extract from a letter, written in 1572, by Christopher Playter to Mr. Kytson, of Hengrove Hall:

'At Chris-time here were certayne masters of defence, that did challenge all comers at all weapons, as long-sworde, staff, sword and buckler, rapier with the dagger: and here were many broken heads, and one of the masters of defence dyed upon the hurt which he received on the head. The challenge was before the quenes Majestie who seemes to have pleasure therein; for when some of them would have sollen a broken pate, her Majesty bade him not to be ashamed to put off his cap, and the blood was spied to run about his face. There was also at the corte new plays which lasted almost all night. The name of the play was huff, suff and ruff, with other masks both of ladies and gents.'

The mention of 'masks' reminds us that it was in Elizabeth's reign that the older pageant – 'enterludes' or 'disgysings' they had been called – turned into the masque: that is to say, plot was added to the mere spectacle which had pleased an earlier age.

It was at a Christmas Feast of Philip and Mary that the first English comedy ever to be performed was acted; and it was at the Inner Temple's 'Grand Christmas' of 1561–62, that the first English tragedy, *Gorboduc*, written by two young members of the Bar, was first played. Elizabeth loved, as did her father, rough and tumble entertainments; if with broken pates and some obvious blood, so much the better; but she was a patroness, at once enthusiastic and admirably competent, of the stage. Theatrical entertainments were a constant source of pleasure to the queen, and it was she herself who, by organizing the presentation of plays, brought the modern stage into being.

In 1569 she formed the Children of the Chapel Royal into a theatrical company under the personal control of Richard Edwards, poet, musician and playwright; and soon after, Elizabeth formed a second company, the Children of the Revels, whose 'star' – immortalized in the beautiful epitaph that Ben Jonson wrote – was a child actor named Salathiel Pavy, who died at the age of thirteen.

These Children of the Revels performed plays by the age's leading writers among them Lyly, Ben Jonson and Shakespeare – and there is a story that Shakespeare himself acted in his own plays, before the Queen.

But the coming of the modern type of stage play, did not, for many years, send the older pageants out of fashion; and the 'masque' with the scripts by Ben Jonson, and 'sets' by Inigo Jones was to come to a period of costly splendour before being killed by the Commonwealth.

In the reign of Elizabeth, England made the decisive change-over from pastoral to being a commercial nation; and the change-over made two classes very powerful – the lawyers and the merchants – so that the Inns of Court and the City's Livery Companies quickly came to be in a position to rival the Crown as patrons of the arts and givers of splendid entertainments, especially at Christmastime.

The Inns of Court were the especial upholders of that curious institution, the Lord of Misrule, though to be sure, he was not neglected by the colleges of the two universities. The Inner Temple, besides appointing a Lord of Misrule to preside over its Christmas junketings ('A repast at dinner is 8*d*'), used to invite some person of great distinction to be the Constable-Marshall for the days of Christmas; and Robert Dudley, afterwards Earl of Leicester, was honoured to accept the appointment of Constable-Marshall for the Christmas of 1561–2. On Boxing Day – then known as St Stephen's Day – he presented himself in Inner Temple hall, 'in gilt armour, with a nest of feathers of all colours on his helm, and a gilt pole-axe in his hand; with him, sixteen trumpeters, four drum and fife, and four men armed from the middle upwards.'

All the sonorous ritual of medieval pageantry was called upon to make these functions as impressive as possible; and to read the Order of Service for the Inner Temple Christmas of that year in which Dudley was Constable-Marshall is to realize how far we have progressed on the road to universal and total drabness!

All 'persons of worship', especially Lieutenants and Sheriffs of counties, kept their Lords of Misrule; and though the Puritans thundered against the custom, even the common people seem to have elected their Christmas Princes or Lords of Misrule; for Parkhurst, Bishop of Norwich, had to issue an injunction in the following terms:

'Item, that no person or persons call themselves lords of misrule in the Christmas tyme, or other vnreuerent* persons at any other tyme, presume to come into church vnreuerently* playing their lewd partes, with scoffing, jesting or ribaldry talke, and if any haue alredy offended herein, to present their names to the ordinery.'

Three persons who were unwise enough to act the parts as bride, bridegroom and parson at a Christmas mock-marriage were sent to repent of their folly in the stocks.

The favourite pastimes of the Queen were dancing and dicing: her luck at the latter being constantly assured by the prudent use of a loaded dice!

National calamities and acts of God – and there were many in Elizabeth's reign – were never considered sufficient reasons, or, indeed, reasons at all, for the Queen's not keeping Christmas, either at Hampton Court, Greenwich or Nonsuch, in royal state.

'The plague', writes Lord Shrewsbury to his Lady in 1568, 'is disposed far abrode in London. So that the Queen kepes hur Kyrsomas her, and goth not to Grenwych, as it was mete.' ('Her' being Hampton Court).

'If ye would,' wrote Sir Thomas Smith from Hampton Court, Christmas 1572, 'what we do here we play at tables, dance and keep Christmas.'

Some of the entertainments of the time strike us in this age as being unnecessarily rough. After the elaborate ritual of St Stephen's Day was ended in the Inner Temple, with the Constable-Marshalls having presided over various ceremonies, 'the Master of the Game standeth up.'

'This ceremony also performed, a Huntsman cometh into the Hall, with a fox and a purse-net; with a cat, both bound at the end of a staff . . .'

It goes on to describe a stomach churning spectacle, and ends with, 'and then proceedeth the second course'! How any of the guests could eat after such 'sport' one cannot, today, imagine.

Queen Elizabeth's Master of Revels was for many years, Sir Thomas Cawarden; and it was he who superintended the plays and pageants of Elizabeth's first Royal Christmas.

An 'economy drive' being ordered by the Queen, Sir Thomas managed to reduce the expenses to £227 11 shillings – £220 less than had been spent the previous Christmas; but these figures were not to remain long at this low level. With the increasing wealth that trade was to bring, the cost of the Christmas entertainments was to be increased at least a hundred times by the beginning of the following reign.

If there is a point at which the Elizabethan Christmas was different from our own it is to be found in the absence of what we might call the 'private' Christmas. All Christmas entertainments were then given for as many persons as possible; and as the poor depended on the Christmas largesse of the noblemen and country gentlemen, Elizabeth passed an act sending the owners back to their estates at Christmas, so that the traditional Christmas entertainment of their tenants should not be allowed to go by default through the absenteeism of their landlords.

Nichols, in his 'Progresses of Queen Elizabeth' tells how, on Twelfth Day, the Lord Mayor, aldermen and all the Crafts of London, and the Batchelors of the Mayors Company, went in procession to St Paul's, 'after the old custom', and there heard a sermon. The same day a stage was set up for a play; and after the play was over a fine 'mask', and afterwards a great banquet which lasted till midnight.

The new rich were building their splendid palaces all over England, designed by such architects as John Thorpe and 'John the Italian' Wilton, Hatfield, Cobham Hall, Penshurst and many other famous houses all dating from this time, and these noble mansions were the scenes of the richest and most elaborate entertainments, especially after Elizabeth had ordered their owners to keep Christmas at home; Ben Jonson has left on record how nobly he was entertained at Penshurst.

Eating was on a grand scale – as it was to remain for nearly four centuries afterwards; and the food was cheap for the poor, so that Christmas was celebrated lavishly by all classes. The Christmas Pudding had not yet made its appearance in history, but its predecessor, plum porridge – a sort of soup made from bread, raisins, sherry, meat, suet, various spices and coloured with saffron – was universally eaten as a ritual dish.

All the same, there had been a marked tendency to simplify the cooking. Boars' Heads, elaborately decorated, were still the *pièce de résistance* of the Christmas Board, but we hear no more of the 'peacock endored' and the other 'subtleties' which were such a feature of the medieval banquet.

Food becomes simpler as its variety increases. There were changes too in the drinking habits of the nation. The art of distilling spirits is supposed to have been invented by the Arabs in the 13th century, and by the end of the 15th century the manufacture of Brandy had become widespread in the wine producing countries. But it was not until the reign of Elizabeth that the use of spirits became general in Britain, and according to Campden, the English troops serving in the Low Countries did much towards introducing the practice in England.

Possibly the bad condition of the Ale may have been responsible for the avidity in which drinkers turned to brandy.

The accent was on good eating and drinking in the days of Good Queen Bess. Elizabeth was much more an autocrat than a bigot; and the acts by which earlier monarchs had sought to forbid card-playing to the lower orders was not found in her reign. She – like all the Tudors – loved card playing, as all other forms of gambling; but she saw no reason to forbid these pleasures to lesser folk. The age then, saw a tremendous rise in the use of playing cards, dicing and other pastimes.

The Christmas Tree had not yet been introduced from Germany. But at Christmas, during Elizabethan times, holly and ivy and other evergreens were hung everywhere. A particular pleasant custom was wreathing of the public monuments in greenery during the days of Christmas.

And that those Elizabethan Christmases were 'merry', there can be no doubt; for the Queen did not think it unworthy of her notice to prevent rises in the cost of those material comforts upon which much of the merriness of Christmas depended.

When in 1591, the powerful Brewers Company sent in a remonstrance against their being compelled to sell beer at a price fixed six years earlier, although every material employed in brewing had greatly increased in price, Elizabeth rejected their protest; and compelled them to withdraw the increased prices that they had taken upon themselves to charge.

The Elizabethans had no 'proprietary' whisky, no cigarettes, no Christmas cards or trees, no coffee, tea or television; but there's no doubt that they had all the ingredients for a right merry Christmas – and of those ingredients they followed the example of their great queen, they made full use of.

'Winter' from Love's Labour's Lost

WILLIAM SHAKESPEARE

When icicles hang by the wall,
And Dick, the Shepherd blows his nail,
And Tom bears logs into the hall,
And milk comes frozen home in pail;

When blood is nipped, and ways be foul,
Then nightly sings the staring owl,
To-whoo;
Tu-whit, to-whoo, a merry note,
While greasy Joan doth keel* the pot

When all aloud the wind doth blow,
And coughing, drowns the parson's saw,
And birds sit brooding in the snow,
  A Marian's nose looks red and raw.

When roasted crabs hiss in the bowl,
Then nightly sings the staring owl,
To-whoo;
Tu-whit, to-whoo, a merry note,
While greasy Joan doth keel* the pot.

*cool

Roasted Crabs & Wassails With 'Carol for the Wassail Bowl'

FROM CHRISTMAS WITH THE POETS

BY THE VITZELLY BROTHERS

In Shakespeare's 'Winter Song', he speaks of the 'Roasted Crabs hissing in the bowl'. The Crabs were little bright red apples, which were grown for their sharp taste when added to other foods, and the high pectin, which was used for preserving and jelling. Their chief use at Christmastide was as an ingredient for the Wassail Bowl. When roasted, they split open to reveal a fluffy whiteness, which spooned on to the spiced ale or cider was called 'Lamb's wool'.

Many ceremonies and traditions were observed. The Wassailers, however poor, had to be welcomed into the house no matter how grand. To refuse them was refusing the good fortune they brought. (Christianity, as well as more ancient custom, also taught that this was the season to give alms to the poor for the cleansing of one's own life or soul.) A few verses were sung before admittance, then the following verses were full of well-wishing and blessings upon the household, ending with a request for alms, which were never refused or they took their good fortune away with them. This was a time of much superstition, and few would take the risk of losing their fortune!

Neither should they refuse to drink from the proffered bowl. The original Wassail is said to have come from a much older custom, whereby enmity was broken and peace signed by the drinking of the Peace Cup – an ale drink. The phrase 'Wassail' comes from the Saxon, 'Wachs Heil', meaning 'I give you health.'

Here is an extract from a piece about the Wassail Bowl, followed by a Wassail song, which may even have been sung at Shakespeare's own front door – it would be certainly most unlikely that he did not know this famous old drinking song, which was sung by groups of maidens carrying around their bowl from house to house over the festive season.

The Boar's Head and the Wassail Bowl were the two most important accessories to Christmas in the olden times, and there are frequent allusions to the latter in the works of our early English poets. The word 'Wassail' occurs in the oldest carol that has been handed down to us, and in extracts from Spenser, Shakespeare and Ben Jonson mention is made of the Wassail Bowl, which shows that in their day, it continued to form a necessary portion of the festivities belonging to the Christmas season. New Year's Eve and Twelfth Night were the occasions on which the Wassail Bowl was chiefly in requisition . . .

While the wealthier classes were enjoying themselves with copious draughts of 'Lamb's wool' – as the beverage, composed of ale, nutmeg, sugar, toast and roasted crabs or apples, with which the bowl was filled, was styled – the poorer people went from house to house with Wassail Bowls adorned with ribbons, singing carols, and inviting those they visited to drink, in return for which little presents of money were generally bestowed upon them.

A Carol for the Wassail Bowl

A Jolly Wassail Bowl
A Wassail of good ale,
Well fare the butler's soul,
That setteth this to sale –
Our Jolly Wassail.

Good Dame, here at your door
Our Wassail we begin,
We are all maidens poor,
We now pray let us in,
With our Wassail.

Our Wassail we do fill
With apples and with spice,
Then grant us your good will,
To taste here once or twice
Of our Wassail

If any maidens be
Here dwelling in this house,
They kindly will agree
To take a full carouse
Of our Wassail.
But here they let us stand
All freezing in the cold;
Good Master, give command
To enter and be bold,
With our Wassail.

Once admitted the Wassailers continue thus:

Much joy into this hall
With us is entered in,
Our Master first of all,
We hope will now begin,
Of our Wassail.

And after, his good Wife
Our spiced bowl will try, –
The Lord prolong your life!
Good fortune we espy,
For our Wassail.

Some Bounty from your hands,
Our Wassail to maintain:
We'll buy no house nor lands
With which we do gain,
With our Wassail.

This is our merry night
Of choosing King and Queen
Then let it be your delight
That something may be seen
In our Wassail.

After the alms have been given:

It is a noble part,
To bear a liberal mind;
God Bless our Master's heart!
For here we comfort find,
With our Wassail.

And now we must be gone,
To seek out more good cheer;
Where bounty will be shown,
As we have found it here.
With our Wassail.

As they leave:

Much joy betide them all,
Our prayers shall be still,
We hope, and ever shall,
For this, your great goodwill
To our Wassail.

My Lorde of Misserule

FROM *THE ANATOMIE OF ABUSES*
BY PHILIP STUBBS

This paper was a rather cynical description of festivals and frivolities of the sixteenth century, giving an accurate if somewhat jaundiced view of the customs of the times. The following describes the 'king' of Twelfth Night, called the Lord of Misrule, whose task it was to 'rule' over the festivities for the duration of the party. There were many ways of electing a king; some chose a card, others picked a piece of cake which had a bean in it, others were elected by popular vote. He would then choose a 'court' of followers, who would do his bidding and adopt silly names and titles. He could be a sensible king, who made sure that the party did not get too out of hand, or he could be quite Bacchanalian, ordering people to do silly things. Some did actually try to attend Church services in this way. They were usually stopped by the clergy, who often hired 'heavies' for the occasion! But those who were powerful enough could not be stopped. In the following description they sound like morris men in fact, although the early mummers and masquers who visited house to house were similar. This is a typical case of three distinct customs becoming combined.

Firste all the wilde heades of the parishe conventynge together, chuse them a grand Capitaine (of mischeef) whom they innoble with the title of my Lorde of Misserule, and hym they crown with great solemnitie, and adopt for their kyng. This kyng anoynted, chuseth for the twentie, fourtie, three score or a hundred lustie guttes like to hymself, to waite uppon his lordely majestie, and to guard his noble persone. Then every one of these his menne he investeth with his liveries of greene, yellowe or some other light wanton colour. And as though that were not baudie enough I should saie, they bedecke themselves with scarffes, ribons, and laces, hanged all over with golde rynges, precious stones, and other jewelles: this doen, they tye about either legge twentie or fourtie belles with rich handkercheefs in their handes, and sometymes laid acrosse over their shoulders and neckes, borrowed for the moste parte of their pretie Mopsies and loovying Bessies, for bussyng them in the darcke.

Thus thinges sette in order, they have their hobbie horses, dragons, and other antiques, together with their baudie pipers, and thunderyng drommers, to strike up the Deville's Daunce withall, and marche these heathen companie towardes the church and churche yarde, their pipers piping, drommers thonderyng, their stumppes dauncyng, their belles iynglyng, their handkerchiefes swyngyng about their heades like madmen, their hobbie horses and other monsters skyrmishyng amongst the throng: and in this sorte they goe to the churche (though the minister bee at praier or preechyng) dauncyng and swingyng their handkercheefes over their heades, in the churche, like devilles incarnate, with suche a confused noise that no man can heare his owne voice. Then the foolishe people, they looke, they stare, they laugh, they fleere, and mount upon formes and pewes, to see these goodly pageauntes, solemnized in this sort.

'The Holly Song'

WILLIAM SHAKESPEARE

Blow, blow, thou Winter Wind,
Thou art not so unkind
As man's ingratitude;
Thy tooth is not so keen,
Because thou art not seen,
Although thy Breath be rude.

Heigh Ho! sing Heigh Ho! unto
the Green Holly:
Most Friendship is feigning, most
loving mere folly;
Then, heigh ho! the Holly!
This life is most Jolly.

Freeze, freeze, thou bitter Sky,
Thou dost not bite so nigh
As benefits forgot:
Though thou the waters warp,
Thy sting is not so sharp
As Friends remembered not.

Heigh Ho! sing Heigh Ho! unto
the Green Holly:

Most Friendship is feigning, most
loving mere folly:
Then, heigh ho!, the Holly!
This life is most Jolly.

To Make a Dish of Snow

FROM *A BOOKE OF COOKERIE*

A recipe for a seasonal-sounding dessert from a late six-teenth-century cookery book entitled **A Book of Cookerie** (1594). Such a book may well have been in the possession of Shakespeare's mother, or even of his wife, and the dish would have been familiar to him.

Take a pottle of sweet thick Cream, and the white of eyght Egs, and beate them altogether, with a spoone, then put them into your cream with a dishfull of Rosewater, and a dishfull of Sugar withall, then take a sticke and make it clene, and then cut it in the end foursquare, and therewith beat all the aforesaid things together, and ever as it ariseth take it off, and put it in to a Cullender, this doone, take a platter and sette an Apple in the midst of it, sticke a thicke bush of Rosemary in the Apple. Then cast your Snow upon the Rosemary and fill your platter therewith, and if you have wafers cast some withall, and so serve them forthe.

'The Christmas Feast'

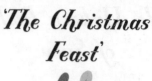

ERIC BENNETT

This is a short discourse on the festive board of the early sixteenth century, by the food writer for the **Tatler** in the 1950s, Eric Bennett. This delicious list of festive foods had evolved from much less palatable fare from the previous century, and was, alas, only to enjoy a short period of success before the Commonwealth arrived with its ensuing problems.

I t was little more than two years before the end of Elizabeth I's reign. The Armada had been defeated, and England was established as a great Power. It was the year Shakespeare wrote *As You Like It*. The year before Spenser died, and Ben Jonson had written *Every Man Out Of His Humour*. It was the climax of a Golden Age in our history. But can one wonder that they wrote so nobly and fought so boldly when they ate so well?

1600. During the sixteenth century the Turkey had been introduced to England, but the Goose was still the favourite bird and the most popular Christmas Dish was Roast Beef.

The Christmas Dinner was still confined to three courses, but the courses had grown more elaborate. The first course might run to thirty-two dishes. Sixteen of them were 'full dishes' (NB, proper recipes as opposed to what we now call 'nibbles').

Shield of Brawn with Mustard, boiled capon, boiled beef, roast beef, roast pork, roasted neats tongues (NB, ox tongue), baked chewets – these were pies containing finely chopped meats with spices – roast goose, roast swan, roast turkey, roast haunch of venison, venison pasty, a kid with pudding in belly, olive pie, roast capons, and a custard. The other sixteen were salads, fricassees and pastries of various kinds.

Fish and Game came with the second course with a choice from cod's head, salmon, smelts, shrimps, lobsters, prawns, sturgeon, woodcock, snipes, smews, and lark pie.

The sweets had become more recognizably Christmassy. In addition to fruit jellies and syllabubs, there were minc'd pies, Christmas pie, and plum porridge.

Plum porridge was a plum pudding cooked without a cloth and served in a tureen. Christmas Pie was a formidable dish, according to one recipe, ' it is a most learned mixture of neats tongues, chicken, eggs, sugar, raising, lemon and orange peel, and various kinds of spicery'.

Strong ale was still a favourite drink. It was no longer all home brewed; there were twenty-six breweries in London alone. The hot spiced ale of the Wassail Bowl was still popular, though now it was known as 'Lambs Wool'.

Home-made cherry brandy and cordials were preferred to wine, but sack-posset, made from hot milk curdled with Canary wine, or sherry was the stuff to get the party going – as Falstaff well knew!

'A Tale of a Merrie Christmas Caroll'

FROM PASQUIL'S *JESTS*

This story of carol singers, found in Pasqil's **Jests** and published in 1609, shows the humour of the time and might even have been told in Christmas company during Shakespeare's seasons in London. As the former Queen Elizabeth I had placed such importance on the lords going home to their estates for Christmas with their tenants, maybe this story was an endorsement of her wishes. This tale has, in Victorian times, been linked to a poetic legend about the Squire of Gamwell Hall in the twelfth century. Whether the poet used the tale recorded in Pasquil, or whether Pasquil used a much older tale to tell I have not been able to find out.

There was sometime an old knight, who being disposed to make himself merry in a Christmas time, sent for many of his tenants and poore neighbours, with their wives, to dinner; when, having made meat to be set on the table, would suffer no man to drinke, till he that was master ouer his wife should sing a carroll, to excuse all the company. Greate nicenesse there was, who should bee the musician, now the cuckow time was so farre off. Yet, with much adoe, looking one upon another, after a dry hemme or two, a dreaming companion drew out as much as hee durst, towards an ill-fashioned ditty.

When having made an end, to the great comfort of the beholders, at last it came to the women's table, where, likewise, commandment was given, that there should no drinke bee touched till she that was master ouer her husband had sung a Christmas carroll; whereupon they fell all to such a singing, that there was never heard such a catterwalling peece of musicke; whereat the knight laughed heartily that it did him half as much good as a corner of his Christmas pie!

'Now Thrice Welcome Christmas!'

GEORGE WITHER

Now thrice welcome Christmas,
Which brings us good cheer,
Minc'd pies and Plum Porridge,
Good Ale and strong Beer;
With Pig, Goose & Capon,
The best that can be;
So well doth the weather
And our Stomachs agree.
Observe how the Chimneys
Do smoke all about,
The cooks are providing
For dinner, no doubt;
But those on whose tables
No Victuals appear,
O, may they keep Lent
For the rest of the Year!
With Holly and Ivy
So green and so gay,
We deck up our Houses
As fresh as the Day.
With Bays and Rosemary,
And Laurel complete;
And everyone now is a King in conceit.

Shakespeare's 'Popish Kingdom'

FROM A TRANSLATION OF THE GERMAN
BY BARNABY GOOGE

Despite its title, the following account in blank verse by Barnaby Googe, 1570, gives an excellent picture of the customs associated with Christmas in Elizabethan England, especially those traditionally observed by the young. Here are described carolling, looking for a husband, divining his characteristics; a rather muddled idea of the observances of the Christmas Mass and Church customs of Christmas Eve and Day; then the custom of blood letting of horses on St Stephen's Day (26 December), St John's Day when it was believed that to eat blessed wine and cake would grant them health during the coming year, and Holy Innocents which was traditionally a day of fasting, chastisement and penitence. This was followed by New Year with its gifts and parties which began on this day and continued through to Twelfth Night. There were customs common to every household:

Twelfth Eve King, the university customs of the Christmas Prince, the Twelfth Night cake with its token which when found makes the finder king for the evening and the house blessings and the blessing of the Senses to keep them good and pure – which in earlier times when village communities were smaller, would have been done by the parish priest, but by Shakespeare's day were done by the master of the household. All are disreputed, yet preserved for posterity in Googe's verse.

Shakespeare was born into a time of religious upheaval. His father was a known recusant, a follower of the old Roman Catholic faith banned by Henry VIII. It is thought that his mother, Mary Arden, was also a recusant, which would explain how a tenant could ask for his Lord's daughter's hand in marriage. The ancient and wealthy Catholic Ardens preferred to have a lowly son-in-law of the same faith than any other in those troubled times. For a while under Queen Mary, and during the early days of Elizabeth's reign, they would have been able to practise their faith openly, but their children would have had to be brought up in the established Church, at least officially. Most recusant families brought their children up in the old faith in secret, so it is probable that William was at least nominally a follower of the old faith in his youth. Therefore, the writing of those such as Barnaby Googe would have been both an annoyance and an amusement to him. In his fanaticism, Googe little realized that he was guilty of keeping alive the memory of Christmas customs which otherwise might have died out completely.

As a man, Shakespeare himself, as far as we know, followed the English Church established by King Henry, which for many people did not seem to be so far removed from the old religion. There was, already, evidence of Puritan development, which was coming across to Britain from North-Western Europe. One advocate of this tide of puritanical teaching was Thomas Kirchmaier, a German writer in 1553, whose book, **Regnum Papisticum** was translated as **The Popish Kingdom** by Barnaby Googe in 1570. Below is his description of Christmas under Queen Elizabeth I and if one looks beyond the sourness of the description there are several references to traditional customs of the time, and one or two which the young Will might have participated in around his neighbours' houses in Stratford-upon-Avon.

Three weeks before the day whereon was born the Lord of grace,
And on the Thursday boys and girls do run in every place,
And bounce and beat at every door, with blows and lusty snaps
And cry, the advent of the Lord, not born as yet, perhaps:
And wishing to the neighbours all, that in the houses dwell,
A happy year and everything to spring and prosper well:
Here have they pears and plums, and pence, each man gives
    willingly,
For these three nights are always thought unfortunate to be:
Wherein they are afraid of sprites and cankered witche's spite,
And dreadful devils, black and grim, that then have chiefest
    might.

In these same days young wanton girls that meet for marriage be,
Do search to know the names of them, that shall their hus-
    bands be.
Four onions, five or eight they take, and make in every one
Such names as they do fancy most, and best do think upon.
Thus near the chimney then they set, and that same onion than
The first doth sprout doth surely bear the name of their good man.
Their husband's nature eke they seek to know, and all his guise;
When as the sun hath hid himself, and left the starry skies,
Unto some woodstack do they go, and while they there do stand,
Each one draws out a faggot stick, the next that comes to hand,

Which if straight and even be, and have no knots at all,
A gentle husband then they think shall surely to them fall.
But if it foul and crooked be, and knotty here and there,
A crabbed churlish husband then they earnestly do fear.

These things the wicked Papists bear, and suffer willingly,
Because they neither do the end, nor fruits of faith espie:
And rather had the people should obey their foolish lust,
Than truly God to know, and in him here alone to trust.
Then comes the day wherein the Lord did bring his birth to pass,
Whereas at midnight up they rise, and every man to mass.
This time so holy counted is, that divers earnestly
Do think the waters all to wine are changed suddenly:
In that same hour that Christ himself was born, and came
    to light
And unto water straight again transformed and altered quite.

There are beside that mindfully the money still do watch,
The first to altar comes, which then they privily do snatch.
The priests lest other should it have takes oft the same away,
Whereby they think throughout the year to have good luck
    in play,
And not to lose: then straight at game till daylight do they strive,
To make some present proof how well their hallowed pence
    will thrive.
Three masses every priest doth sing upon that solemn day,
With offerings unto everyone, that so the more may play.

This done, a wooden child in clouts is on the altar set,
About the which both boys and girls do dance, and trimly jet,
And carols sing in praise of Christ, and for to help them here,
The organ answers every verse, with sweet and solemn cheer.
The priests do roar aloud, and round about the parents stand,

To see the sport, and with their voice do help them and their hand.
Thus wont the Coribants perhaps upon the mountain Ide,
The crying noise of Jupiter new born with song to hide,
To dance about him round, and on their brazen pans to beat,
Lest that his father finding him, should him destroy and eat.
Then following Saint Stephen's Day, whereon doth every man
His horses jaunt and course abroad, as swiftly as he can.
Until they do extremely sweat, and then they let them blood,
For this being done upon this day, they say doth do them good,
And keep them from all maladies and sickness through the year,
As if that Stephen any time took charge of horses here.

Next John the son of Zebedee hath his appointed day,
Who once by cruel tyrants will constrained was, they say,
Strong poison up to drink, and therefore the Papists do believe,
That whoso puts their trust in him, no poison can them grieve.
The wine beside that hallowed is, in worship of his name,
The priests do give the people that bring money for the same.
And after with the selfsame wine are little manchets made,
Against the boistrous winter storms, and sundry suchlike trade;
The men upon this solemn day do take this holy wine,
To make them strong, so do the maids, to make them fair
    and fine.

Then comes the day that calls to mind the cruel Herod's strife,
Who, seeking Christ to kill, the King of everlasting life,
Destroyed the infants young, a beast unmerciless,
And put to death all such as were of two years old or less.
To them the sinful wretches cry, and earnestly do pray,
To get them pardon for their faults, and wipe their sins away.
The parents when this day appears, do beat their children all
(Though nothing they deserve), and servants all to beating fall.
And monks do whip each other well, or else their prior great,

Or Abbot mad, doth take in hand their breeches all to beat.
In worship of these innocents, or rather as we see,
In honour of the cursed king who did this cruelty.

The next to this is New Year's Day, whereon to every friend
They costly presents in do bring and New Year's gifts do send.
These gifts the husband gives his wife and father eke the child,
And master on his men bestows the like, with favours mild,
And good beginning of the year they wish and wish again,
According to the ancient guise of heathen people vain,
These eight days no man doth require his debts of any man,
Their tables they do furnish out with all the meat they can:
With marchpanes, tarts, and custards great they drink with
    staring eyes,
They rout and revel, feed and feast, as merry as the pies,
As if they should at the entrance of this New Year have to die,
Yet would they have their bellies full and ancient friends ally.

The wise men's day here followeth, who out from Persia far,
Brought gifts and presents unto Christ, conducted by a star.
The Papists do believe that these were kings, and so them call,
And do affirm that of the same there were but three in all.
Here sundry friends together come, and meet in company,
And make a king amongst themselves by voice or destiny;
Who after princely guise appoints his officers alway,
Then unto feasting do they go, and long time after play:
Upon their Boards in order thick the dainty dishes stand,
Till that their purses empty be and creditors at hand.
Their children herein follow them, and choosing princes here
With pomp and great solemnity they meet and make good cheer
With money either got by stealth, or of their parents eft,
That so they may be trained to know both riot here and theft.
Then every householder to his ability,

Doth make a mighty cake, that may suffice his company:
Herein a penny doth he put, before it comes to fire,
This he divides according to his household doth require;
And every piece distributeth, as round about they stand
Which in their names unto the poor is given out of hand;
But whoso chanceth on the piece wherein the money lies
Is counted king amongst them all, and is with shouts and cries
Exhalted to the heavens up, who taking chalk in hand,
Doth make a cross on every beam and rafters as they stand:
Great force and power have these against all injuries and harms
Of cursed devils, sprites and bugs, of conjuring and charms.
So much this king can do, so much the crosses bring to pass,
Made by some servant, maid or child, or by some foolish ass.

Twice six nights then from Christmas do they count with
    diligence,
Wherein each master in his house doth burn up frankincense :
And on the table sets a loaf, when night approacheth near,
Before the coals, and frankincense be perfumed there:
First bowing down his head he stands, and nose and ears and eyes,
He smokes, and with his mouth receives the fume that doth arise:
Whom followeth straight his wife, and doth the same full
    solemnly,
And of their children every one, and all their family:
Which doth preserve, they say, their teeth, and nose and eyes
    and ear,
From every kind of malady, and sickness all the year.
When every one received hath this odour great and small,
Then one takes up the pan with coals, and frankincense and all
Another takes the loaf, whom all the rest do follow here,
And round the house they go, with torch or taper clear,
That neither meat do want, nor witch with dreadful charm
Have power to hurt their children, or to do their cattle harm.

There are that three nights only to perform this foolish gear,
To this intent, and think themselves safe all year.
To Christ dare none commit himself. And in these days beside
They judge what weather all the year shall happen and betide:
Ascribing to each day a month, and at this present time
The youth in every place do flock, and all appareled fine,
With pipers through the streets they run, and sing at every door
In commendation of the man rewarded well therefore,
Which on themselves they do bestow, or on the church as tho'
The people were not plagued with rogues and begging friars
    enow.

There cities are where boys and girls together still do run,
About the street with like, as soon as night begins to come,
And bring abroad their wassail bowls, who well rewarded be
With cakes and cheese and great good cheer and money
    plenteously.

The Order of Christmas

AN ACCOUNT OF CHRISTMAS

AT THE COURT OF ELIZABETH

FROM DUGDALE'S *ORIGINES JURIDICIALES*

Extracts from Sir William Dugdale's **Origines Juridiciales** (1666) of the daily arrangements and the duties of the various officers and servants during the twelve days of Christmas at the Court of Queen Elizabeth some eighty to one hundred years earlier are reproduced here. Copies (near complete) in English are reproduced in a number of works, including the Christmas reference works of Dawson (1903) and John Ashton (1893).

First it hath been the duty of the Steward to produce five fat Brawns, Vessels, Wood, and other necessities belonging to the kitchen; as also all manner of Spices, Flesh, Fowl, and other Cates for the kitchin.

The office of the chief Butler to provide a rich cupboard of Plate, Silver and Parcel-gilt; seaven dozen of Silver and Parcel-gilt spoons; twelve fair Saltcellars, likewise Silver and Gilt; Twenty Candlesticks of the like.

Twelve fine large Tablecloths of Damask and Diaper, Twenty dozen of Napkins suitable at the least. Three dozen of fair large Towells; whereof the Gentlemen Sewers and Butlers of the house, to have every of them one at meal-times, during their attendance. Likewise to provide carving knives; twenty dozen of white Cups and green Potts; a Carving Table; Torches; Bread; Beer, and Ale. And the chief of the Butlers was to give attendance on the highest Table in the Hall, with Wine, Ale, and Beer; and all the other Butlers to attend at the other tables in like sort.

The Cupboard of Plate is to remain in the Hall on Christmas Day, St. Stephan's Day and New Yeare's Day. Upon the Banquetting night it was removed to the Butry; which in all respects was very laudably performed.

The office of the Constable Marshall to provide for his employment, a fair gilt compleat Harneys, with a nest of Fethers in the Helm; a fair Poleaxe to bear in his hand, to be chevalrously ordered on Christmas Day and other days, as afterwards is shewed; touching the ordering and settling of all which ceremonies, during the said Grand Christmas, a solemn consultation was held at their Parliament* in the House; in the form following:

First, at the Parliament kept in their Parliament Chamber in this House, on the Even at Night of St. Thomas the Apostle, Officers are to attend, according as they have been long before that time, at a former Parliament, named and elected to undergo several offices for this time of solemnity, honour, and pleasance; of which officers these are the most emminent; namely, the Steward, Marshall, Constable Marshall, Butler, and Master of the Game.

These Officers are made known and elected in Trinity Term next before; and to have knowledge thereof by letters, in the country, to the end they may prepare themselves against

All-Hallow-tide; that, if such nominated officers happen to fail, others may then be chosen in their rooms. The other Officers are appointed at other times nearer Christmas Day.

Christmas Eve. – The Marshall at dinner is to place at the highest Table's end, and next to the Library, all on one side thereof, and most antient persons in the company present: the Dean of the Chappel next to him; then an antient of Bencher, beneath him. At the other end of the table, the Sewer, Cupbearer, and Carver. At the upper end of the Bench-table, the King's Searjeant and Chief Butler; and when the Steward hath served in, and set on the table the first mess, then he is also to sit down.

The order of seating continues with the Master of Revels, the Ranger, Master of Game, etc. down to the Clerk of the Souse tub even! Then begins the ritual of table dressing with the silver plate, linens and salts, trenchers and bread, all in the correct order of laying. A modern student of 'silver service' does not know how easy the order of service is now compared with that of Shakespeare's time.

At the first course the Minstrells must sound their instruments, and go before; and the Steward and Marshall are next to follow together; and after them the Gentleman Sewer; and then cometh the meat. Those three officers are to make together three solemn courtesies, at three several times, between the Skreen and the upper Table; and the second at the midst; and the third at the other end; and then standing by the Sewer performeth his Office.

Whilst the tables are set according to strict ritual, there was: Musick must stand at the Harth side, with the noise of their Musick, their faces direct towards the highest Table; and that done, to return to the Butry with their Musick sounding.

This ritual followed for the second course also, the music now becoming more pervasive after the eating, with songs as well as music.

Then after a little repose, the persons at the highest table arise and prepare to revells: in which time, the Butlers, and other Servitors with them, are to dine in the Library. At both the doors of the Hall are Porters to view the comers in and out at Meal times; to each of them is allowed a cast of Bread and a Caudle nightly after Supper.

At Night before Supper there are Revells and Dancing, and so also after Supper during the twelve daies of Christmass; the antientest Master of the Revells is, after Dinner and Supper, to sing a Caroll or Song; and command other Gentlemen then there present to sing with him and the Company, and so it is very decently performed.

A repast at Dinner is eight pence.

Christmass Day – Service in the Church ended, the Gentlemen presently repair into the Hall to Breakfast, with Brawn, Mustard and Malmsey.

The description of laying the tables for dinner continues in much the same vein as before.

At the first course, is served a fair and large Bore's-head upon a Silver Platter, with Minstralsye. Two Gentlemen in Gowns are to attend at Supper, and to bear two fair Torches of Wax next before the Musicians and Trumpetters, and to stand above the Fire with the Musick till the first Course be served in through the Hall. Which performed they, with the Musick, are to return to the Butry. The like course is to be observed in all things, during the time of Christmass. The like at Supper.

A repast at Dinner is twelve shillings.

Then there follows another religious service after dinner. Christmas Day being more solemn than the days which follow.

St. Stephen's Day – This day the Steward, Carver and Cup-Bearer are to serve as afore. After the first course served in, the Constable-Marshall cometh into the Hall, arrayed with fair rich compleat Harneys, white and bright, and gilt, with a nest of Fethers of all colours upon his Crest or Helm, and a gilt Poleaxe in his hand: to whom is associate the Lieutenant of the Tower, armed with a fair white Armour, a nest of Fethers in his Helm, and a like Poleaxe in his hand; and with them sixteen trumpetters; four Drums and Fifes going in rank before them; and with them attendeth four men in white Harneys, from the middle upwards, and Halberds in their hands, bearing on their shoulders the Tower: which persons with the Drums, Trumpetts and Musick, go three times about the Fire. Then the Constable-Marshall, after two or three curtesies made, kneeleth down before the Lord Chancellor; behind him the Lieutenant; and they kneeling, the Constable Marshall pronounceth an oration of a quarter of an hour's length, thereby declaring the purpose of his coming; and that his purpose is to be admitted into his Lordship's service.

Then cometh the Master of the Game, apparelled in green Velvet, and the Ranger of the Forest also, in a green Suit of Satten; bearing in his hand a green Bow and divers Arrows, with wither of them a Hunting Horn about their necks; blowing together three blasts of venery, they pace around the Fire three times. Then the Master of the Game maketh three courtesies, as aforesaid.

Then proceedeth the second course.

At Supper the Hall is to be served with all solemnity, as upon Christmasday. Supper ended, the Constable-Marshall presenteth hisself with Drums afore him, mounted upon a

Scaffold, born by four Men, and goeth three times about the Harth, crying out loud, 'A Lord, A Lord' etc. then he decendeth and goeth to dance etc., and after he calleth his Court every one by name, one by one in this manner:

Sir Francis Flatterer of Fowlshurst in the County of Buckingham.

Sir Randle Rakabite, of Rascall-hall, in the County of Rakehell.

Sir Morgan Mumchance, of Much Monkery, in the County of Mad Mopery.

Sir Bartholomew Balbreech, of Buttocksbury, in the County of Brekenock.

This done the Lord of Misrule addresses himself to the Banquet: which ended with some Minstralsye, Mirth and Dancing, every Man departeth to rest.

Every repast is six pence.

Here it should be explained to those not initiated into the mysteries of the Christmas Revels that the ceremony described above is the beginning of the fun and games part of Christmas, the religious observances over for the time being. The Constable Marshal has announced who his Revels Court will be and given them the outlandish names, by which characters he wishes them to behave. This 'Court' will preside over all the revels now until Twelfth Night.

To Make Buttered Oranges

A CHRISTMAS DESSERT RECIPE

Oranges were an expensive fruit and the following sixteenth/early seventeenth-century recipe might have been a special Christmas dessert.

Take a pint of Creame, raspe the peels of two Oranges into half a pint of water or Orange juice, six eggs, two whites, as much suger as will sweeten it, straine and set over a fire. When it is thick put a piece of Butter as big as a Egg and keep it stirring till cold.

'December' Sonnet

WILLIAM SHAKESPEARE

In his sonnets Shakespeare tells of a lover's longings, likening them to the fair days of spring and summer, and the sadness of parting and absence like the days of winter. Here is a short verse describing the feelings of December.

How like a winter hath my absence been
From thee, the pleasure of the fleeting year!
What freezings have I felt, what dark days seen!
What old December's bareness everywhere!
And yet this time remov'd was summer's time,
The teeming autumn, big with rich increase,
Bearing the wanton burdon of the prime . . .

The Order of Christmas Continued

FROM DUGDALE'S *ORIGINES JURIDICIALES*

This is a continuation of the 'Order of Christmas' from Dugdale's *Origines Juridiciales*; the following days describe the more riotous 'revells' of Shakespeare's England. Included are some notes as to the origins and meanings of the customs.

St. John's Day – About seaven of the clock in the morning, the Lord of Misrule is abroad, and if he lacks any Officer or Attendant, he repaireth to their Chambers, and compelleth them to attend in person upon him after Service in the Church, to Breakfast, with Brawn, Mustard and Malmsey. After Breakfast ended, his Lordship's power is in suspense, until his personal presence at night; and then his power is most potent.

After the second course (of Dinner), the King's Searjant, orator-like, declareth the disorder of the Constable-Marshall, and the Common Searjant; who defendeth himself and Constable-Marshall, with words of great efficacy. Hereto the King's Searjant replyeth. They rejoyn etc. and who so is found faulty is committed to the Tower etc.

This ceremony follows an ancient pre-Christian custom of electing a scapegoat as 'King', allowing him all honours, then sacrificing him, in the belief that in dying with all honours he is taking all the ills of the people with him. In Shakespeare's time, the 'king' or in this case, the Constable-Marshall, is given a mock trial, and committed to the Tower, but is not really sent there but to the tower 'corner' where stand the four model Tower Bearers.

If any officer be found absent from Dinner or Supper; if it be complained of, he that sitteth in his place is adjudged to have like punishment as the Officer should have been present: and then withall he is enjoyned to supply the office of the true absent Officer, in all pointe. If any Offender escape from the Lieutenant into the Butry, and bring into the Hall a Manchet of Bread upon the point of a Knife, he is pardoned: for the Buttry in that case is Sanctuary. After Cheese is served to the Table not any is commanded to sing.

Childermas Day [Now known as Holy Innocents].

In the Morning, as afore, the Hall is served; saving that the Sewer, Carver, and Cup-Bearer, do not attend any Service. Also like Ceremony at Supper.

New Year's Eve – At Breakfast, Brawn, Mustard & Malmsey. At Dinner, Roast Beef, Venison Pasties, with like solemnities as afore. And at Supper, Mutton, and Hens roasted.

New Year's Day – In the morning, Breakfast as formerly. At Dinner, like solemnity as at Christmas Eve.

From this we see that the present custom of New Year is newer than that observed in Shakespeare's time.

The Banquetting Night.

This is most likely to have been the eve of Twelfth Day,
which was the traditional time for the activities which are
following described. While many of Shakespeare's plays
were performed on the other days of Christmas, notably
St Stephen's Day, which we now call 'Boxing Day,' and Holy
Innocent's Day, the traditional time, when most of his plays
were probably performed, was in fact Twelfth Eve. Plays,
particularly the Comedies, were most popular during the
reign of Queen Elizabeth, while King James who followed
her preferred the Masques.

It is proper to the Butlers Office to give warning to every
House of Court, of this Banquet; to the end that they, and
the Innes of Chancery, be invited thereto to see a Play and
Mask. The Hall is to be furnished with Scaffolds to sit on,
for Ladies to behold the Sports, on each side. Which ended,
the Ladies are to be brought into the Library, unto the
Banquet there; and a table is to be covered and furnished
with all Banquetting Dishes, for the Lord Chancellor, in the
Hall; where he is to call to him the Ancients of the other
Houses, as many as may be on one side of the Table. The
Banquet is to be served by the Gentlemen of the House.

The Marshall and Steward are to come before the Lord
Chancellor's mess. The Butlers for Christmas must serve
Wine; and the Butlers of the House Beer and Ale, etc.
When the Banquet is ended, then cometh into the Hall the
Constable-Marshall, fairly mounted on his Mule; and devi-
seth some Sport for passing away the rest of the Night.

Twelfth Day – At Breakfast, Brawn, Mustard and
Malmsey, after Morning Prayer ended. And at Dinner, the
Hall is to be served as upon St. John's Day.

'The Burning
Babe'

FATHER ROBERT SOUTHWELL, MARTYR

Religious persecution, begun in Henry VIII's reign, was at its height in the years during Shakespeare's life. Elizabeth, otherwise so sensible and just in her preoccupation with the healthy and fair living of her people, was remarkably harsh concerning religion. Robert Southwell was born four years before Shakespeare and was sent abroad at an early age to be educated. At the age of twenty-four he came back to England as a priest ministering to the persecuted Catholics who were not allowed to practise their religion under pain of death. Southwell found time to write a number of poems before he was caught, tortured and executed at Tyburn on 21 February 1595, aged only thirty-two years. 'The Burning Babe' was written during his last Christmas/winter season in prison, 1594–5, as part of a group of poems called 'Moeoniae'. It was a theological poem which was later praised by Ben Jonson, who said that he would have been content to destroy many of his own writings if he had written 'The Burning Babe'. Southwell also wrote 'New Heaven, New War', a long poem from which Benjamin Britten took several verses to set to music:

This little Babe, so few days old
Is come to rifle Satans fold.
All Hell doth at His presence quake,
Though he himself from cold do shake.

Father Southwell's martyrdom was notorious in London
that year and Shakespeare would certainly have been familiar with his poems, the story behind the man and the news
of his execution. Many poets and playwrights of the day
made comment about the worth of the man. We have no
record that Shakespeare was one of them, but perhaps as
his contemporaries and friends spoke of Southwell with
affection, Shakespeare did too!

As I in a hoary Winter's night stood shivering in the snow,
Surprised I was with sudden heat which made my heart
    to glow;
And lifting up a fearful eye to view what fire was near,
A pretty Babe all burning bright did in the air appear.
As though his floods should quench his flames with what His
    tears were fed;
Alas, quoth He, but newly born in fiery heats I fry,
Yet none approach to warm their hearts or feel my fire but I.
My faultless breast the furnace is, the fuel is wounding thorns,
Love is the fire, and sighs the smoke, the ashes shame and
    scorns;
The fuel Justice layeth on, and Mercy blows the coals;
The metal in this furnace wrought are men's defiled souls
For which, as now on fire I am, to work them to their good,
So will I melt into a bath, to wash them in my blood
With this, He vanished, out of sight, and swiftly shrunk away
And straight I called unto mind that this was Christmas Day.

How to Make Benicryz

ADAPTED FROM THE ORIGINAL RECIPE

MARIA HUBERT

Benicryz, or 'benicrz' as I have also seen it spelled, is a delicious mini doughnut-type of dessert, which was popular throughout the seventeenth century and probably earlier. There are similar street sweets served in Spain called Churros and Roscos – the latter containing sherry – which were originally served at the great feasts, including the Feast of Holy Cross. I do not profess to know the origin of the name Benicrz, but 'Beni' could be a corruption of the Spanish or Latin words for 'good' and 'crz' could possibly be a corruption of 'cruz', or 'cross'. The recipe appears in several manuscripts and printed cookery books of the late sixteenth and seventeenth centuries. It was a popular snack at the street fairs of Elizabethan and Jacobean England, when one could buy a portion freshly fried to eat hot. Perhaps it may have been one of the sweets served to play-goers. The archaic language of the original recipe has been modernized here so that readers who wish to try the recipe can do so more easily!

Take six tablespoonfuls of flour (plain); grate a little nutmeg into it and a pinch of salt, put in a tablespoonful of sweet sherry, and mix it with milk, as thick as for pancakes. Leave for a few minutes while you melt butter into a pan (non-stick for best results today), and pour just enough of the mixture to make a very thin pancake. Let it set but not brown.

When they are all made thus, our seventeenth-century housewife would beat them in a mortar (perhaps a mixer, or better still a food processor, would be today's equivalent), adding six eggs, one at a time.

Heat beef suet (or oil) in a large deep pan and put in a knife's blade of the mixture at a time to fry quickly. Now we may quote from our original recipe for the authentic finale:

When lightly browned take them out of the liquid with a slice and set them in a cullender before the fire (to keepe warme and drain off of the fat). The quicker you serve them the better, grate sugar over them very thick and serve them up.

Mysteries, Minstrels & Puppets

THE STREET PLAYS OF SHAKESPEARE'S TIME
WITH 'A HYMN OF THE NATIVITY SUNG BY THE
SHEPHERDS' BY RICHARD CRASHAW, C. 1630

The mystery plays known to Shakespeare were not the same as those we are familiar with today. In Elizabethan England a mystery was a telling of one of the stories from the Bible. These were originally performed by the guilds, who were most solicitous of their own parts, and they were performed on 'floats', movable carts, which were set up in different parts of the town. The popular scene of the Massacre of the Holy Innocents in the mystery plays from Coventry, which was very close to Stratford, was the prerogative of the Shearers and Taylors Guild.

These plays were also performed at fairs by travelling showmen, who used puppets, a custom which lasted well into the twentieth century in parts of Europe, notably Italy and Poland. Such sights were also familiar to the Bard who refers to them briefly in The Winter's Tale.

The third group to work with the mysteries were the minstrels and the poets. They would write verses with individual parts to be sung to an audience, usually of a house party. The shepherds were the most popular character for this entertainment, and such songs could be performed by invitation or by gatecrashing – as did Henry VIII in Shakespeare's play of the same name, when Henry and a group of maskers gatecrash Wolsey's house party, dressed as shepherds (Act I, sc. iv).

The following is a part song of the shepherds written by Richard Crashaw, 1612–49. Born of Puritan parents, he was educated at Charterhouse and Cambridge and became a Catholic in the middle years of his short life.

A HYMN OF THE NATIVITY
SUNG BY THE SHEPHERDS

Come, we shepherds whose blest sight
Hath met Love's noon in Nature's night;
Come, lift we up our loftier song,
And wake the sun that lies too long.
To all our world of well-stol'n joy
He slept, and dreamt of no such thing,
While we found out Heaven's fairer eye,
And kiss'd the cradle of our King;
Tell him he rises now too late
To show us aught worth looking at.

Tell him we now can show him more
Than he e'er showed a mortal sight,
Than he himself e'er saw before,
Which to be seen needs not his light:

Tell him, Tityrus, where thou' hast been,
Tell him Thyrsis, what thou hast seen.

TITYRUS:
Gloomy night embraced the place
Where the noble infant lay;
The babe look'd up and showed his face;
In spite of darkness it was day.
It was Thy day, sweet, and did rise,
Not from the East but from thy eyes.
CHORUS: It was Thy day, sweet ...

THYRSIS:
Winter chid aloft, and sent
The angry North to wage his wars:
The North forgot his fierce intent,
And left perfumes instead of scars.
By those sweet eyes' persuasive powers,
Where he meant frosts he scattered flowers.
CHORUS: By those sweet eyes' ...

BOTH:
We saw Thee in Thy balmy nest,
Young dawn of our eternal day;
We saw Thine eyes break from the East,
And chase the trembling shades away:
We saw Thee, and we blest the sight,
We saw Thee by Thine own sweet light.
CHORUS: We see Thee, ...

TITYRUS:
Poor world said I, what wilt thou do
To Entertain this starry stranger?

Is this the best thou can'st bestow –
A cold and not too cleanly manger?
Contend, the powers of heaven and earth,
To fit a bed for this huge birth.
CHORUS: Contend, the powers . . .

THYRSIS:
Proud world, said I, cease your contest,
And let the mighty babe alone,
The phoenix builds the phoenix's nest,
Love's architecture is His own.
The babe, whose birth embraves this morn,
Made His own bed e'er He was born.
CHORUS: The babe, whose birth . . .

TITYRUS:
I saw the curls drops, soft and slow,
Come hovering o'er the place's head,
Off'ring their whitest sheets of snow,
To furnish the fair infant's bed.
Forbear, said I be not too bold,
Your fleece is white, but 'tis too cold.
CHORUS: Forbear, said I . . .

THYRSIS:
I saw the obsequious seraphim
Their rosy fleece of fire bestow,
For well they now can spare their wings
Since Heaven itself lies here below.
Well done, said I: but are you sure
Your down soft warm, will pass for pure?
CHORUS: Well done, said I . . .

BOTH:
No, no, your King's not yet to seek
Where to repose His royal head;
See, see how soon His new-bloom'd cheek
'Twixt mother's breasts is gone to bed.
Sweet choice, said we, no way but so,
Not to lie cold, yet sleep in snow!
CHORUS: Sweet choice . . .

FULL CHORUS:
Welcome all wonders in one sight!
Eternity shut in a span!
Summer in winter! Day in night!

CHORUS:
Heaven in earth! and God in man!
Great little one, whose all-embracing birth
Lifts earth to heaven, stoops heaven to earth!

To Thee meek Majesty, soft King
Of simple graces and sweet loves!
Each of us his lamb will bring
Each his pair of silver doves!
At last, in fire of Thy fair eyes,
Ourselves become our own best sacrifice.

Shakespeare's Christmas Dinner

AND *CHRISTMAS HUSBANDLY FARE*

BY THOMAS TUSSER

What festive fare would Shakespeare have enjoyed, as a boy growing up in Stratford-upon-Avon and as a man, when many of his Christmases were spent in London entertaining the Queen and her royal court with one of his plays such as *Measure for Measure*, which was first performed at court on 26 December 1604. Doubtless he would have enjoyed more elegant food than his wife would have provided, even at the height of his popularity. Christmas fare tended to be as varied then as it is now. Some families would have eaten the good roast beef of old England, others would have preferred brawn. If you were at Oxford University, you would have feasted on boar's head with mustard, of which brawn, made from the meat of a pig's head, is a descendant. A few had already succumbed to the new fashionable meat recently brought from the Americas and said to be the favourite Christmas dish of Queen Elizabeth I – the turkey. Mince pies were made with real meat, usually shredded tongue, and the spices were symbolic of the Holy Land, where Jesus was born. The original spices were brought back by crusader knights.

The following poem is by Thomas Tusser, a poet who was already an elderly man when Shakespeare was born. Tusser was a great observer and recorder of the domestic and the natural world around him, and in *Christmas Husbandly Fare*, written in the late sixteenth century, he gives an account of what would have been served in a household such at that in which young Will Shakespeare grew up:

Good Husband and Housewife, now chiefly be glad
Things handsome to have, as they ought to be had,
They both do provide against Christmas do come,
To welcome their neighbour, good cheer to have some;
Good bread and good drink, a good fire in the hall,
Brawn pudding and souse, and good mustard withal;
Beef, mutton, and pork, shred pies of the best,
Pig, veal, goose, and capon, and turkey well dress'd;
Cheese, apples, and nuts, jolly carols to hear,
As then in the country is counted good cheer.

What cost to good husband is any of this,
Good household provision only it is;
Of other the like I do leave out a many,
That costeth the husbandman never a penny.

A very descriptive account of what was considered a 'moderate' dinner of the time is also found in a book on housewifery of the time:

There should be full sixteen dishes at table; that is, dishes of meat that are of substance, and not empty or for show – as thus, for example; first, a shield of

Brawne with Mustarde; secondly a boyl'd Capon; thirdly, a boyl'd piece of Beef; fourthly, a Chine of Beef, rosted; fifthly, a neat's Tongue, rosted; sixthly, a Pig, rosted; seventhly, Chewets, baked; eighthly, a Goose rosted; ninethly, a Swan, rosted; tenthly, a Turkie, rosted; the eleventh, a haunch of Venison, rosted; the twelfth, a pasty of Venison; the thirteenth, a Kid, with a pudding in the belly; the fourteenth, an Olive-pye; the fifteenth, a couple of Capons; the sixteenth, a Custard, or Dowsetts.

Now to these full dishes may be added sallets, fricases, quelque choses, and devised paste, as many dishes more, which make the full service no less than two and thirty dishes; which is as many as can conveniently stand on one table, and in one messe. And after this manner you may proportion both your second and third courses, holding fulness on one half of the dishes, and show on the other; which will be both frugal in the splendour, contentment to the guest, and much pleasure and delight to the beholder.

A Receipt for a Bean Cake

A SIXTEENTH-CENTURY RECIPE

FOR A TWELFTH NIGHT CAKE

This is the late sixteenth-century recipe for a cake for Twelfth Night, such as was made by housewives in Shakespeare's time. There are no records of what Shakespeare's mother, Mary Arden, or his wife, Anne, would have produced for Christmas, but as this recipe was a popular one, it is conceivable that they might have made it. Bean cake appears to have been a kind of gingerbread, and was called peppercake in the Northern counties. It was distinct from Twelfth cake, which was a rich fruit cake, iced and decorated in a manner similar to that of Christmas cake, which is its descendant.

In later years, without its bean, but served with a thin slice of cheese, bean cake used to be given to children and callers at Christmas time, and the following verse is associated with the cake:

A Little bit of Peppercake,
A little bit of cheese,
A cup of cold water

And a penny if you please.

> In the recipe for the bean cake you can omit the pearl ash
> if you wish; it adds little to the flavour really, but for those
> who wish to use it it can generally be purchased in small
> quantities from most dispensing chemists.

Ingredients:
1 lb plain flour
1 teaspoon pearl ash melted in a little lukewarm milk
1 oz powdered cloves
1 lb black treacle
1 teaspoon ground white pepper
1 teaspoon ground ginger
1 lb butter
5 beaten eggs

Mix all ingredients together – you can use a mixer. You will
find it easier if you melt the treacle with the butter and add to
the flour and spices and then add the eggs, in that order. Line
baking tins or cake tins with baking parchment and bake in a
moderate oven (about 160°C for electric) for about two hours.

This is a typical old recipe to make one very large cake.
If you use smaller tins, reduce the baking time accordingly.
The usual cake tests apply, springs back when pressed.
Allow to go cold, and slice thinly. Nice spread with butter,
marmalade, or the traditional cheese.

If you are making a bean cake, wrap the dried bean (I use
dried butter beans) in parchment and put into the dough.
Slice the cake for as many guests as will be eating it, and the
winner of the bean either becomes your King/Queen for the
party, or you can have a small 'unisex' gift ready to bestow!

On Flapdragon

A SUMMARY OF ACCOUNTS OF THE ANCIENT GAME QUOTED BY SHAKESPEARE

Various accounts of the ancient game of Snapdragon, which has been a Christmas pastime certainly from medieval times – or earlier if we are to believe the players in *Lingua* – to the present. Shakespeare was certainly familiar with it, for he brings it into two of his plays; here is how it was acknowledged in Shakespeare's day:

From the play LINGUA, 1607.

MEMORY: O I remember this dish well, it was first invented by Pluto, to intertaine Proserpina withall.
PHANTASTES: – I think not, Memory, for when Heracles had kild the flaming dragon of Hesperdia with the Apples of that Orchard he made this fiery meate; in memory whereof hee named it Snapdragon.

Henry IV, Part II, Act II, sc. iv, Falstaff says that the Prince likes Poins because he:

'... plays at quoits well, eats conger and fennel and drinks off candles's ends for flap-dragons ...'

Can he possibly be referring to the West Country custom, which was not quite the same as the fruit and brandy Snapdragon, in which a lighted candle was placed in a cup of cider or ale and the player had to drink the ale without burning his face? And again the Bard makes reference to the sport in *Love's Labour's Lost* (Act V, sc. i), when Costard, upon encountering a group who are arguing at length, says to Moth, his companion:

'... I marvel thy master has not eaten thee for a word; for thou art not so long, by the head as honorificabilitudinitatibus: thou are easier swallowed than a flap-dragon.'

John Ashton, writing of the Elizabethan sport in 1893, describes it as:

... A kind of game, in which Brandy is poured over a large dish of raisins, and then set alight. The object is to snatch the raisins out of the flames and devour them without burning oneself. This can be managed by sharply seizing them and shutting the mouth at once. It is suggested that the name is derived from the German Snappes, 'spirit' and Drache 'Dragon.'

Sandys, writing in the early 1800s, also makes reference to Shakespeare and Flapdragon:

In juvenile parties, Snap-Dragon, throwing its mysterious and witchlike hue over the faces of the bystanders. Not Poin's who swallowed down candle ends for flap-dragons;

but the veritable Malaga fruit, carolling away in the frolicsome spirit, burning the fingers but rejoicing the palate of the adventurous youth, and half frightened little maiden reveller. The custom is old, but not quite so old as stated in the curious play 'Lingua' by the performance of one character, wherein – Tactus – Oliver Cromwell is said to have had his first dream of ambition.

The Elizabethan love of forfeits and gambling games made Snapdragon, or Flapdragon, a most popular pastime. And several people wrote on its merits or otherwise, and described methods for achieving success. Elizabethan advice repeated in 'Pantalogia' (1813) advised the 'gamsters' thus:

Set fire to the warm brandy in an earthenware bowl, and throw raisins into it. Those who are unused to this sport are afraid to pluck out the fruit, but the raisins may be safely snatched out by a quick motion and put blazing into the mouth which being closed, the fire is at once extinguished. The game requires both courage and rapidity of action, and a good deal of merriment is caused by the unsuccessful efforts of competitors for the raisins in the flaming bowl.

The following verse was traditionally sung by onlookers while the foolhardy tried their luck and their fingers in the dish of flaming fruit.

> Here he comes with flaming Bowle,
> Don't he mean to take hys tolle,
> Snip! Snap! Dragon!

Take care you don't take too much,
Be not greedy in your clutch,
Snip! Snap! Dragon!

With his blue and lappinge Tongue,
Many of you will bee stung,
Snip! Snap! Dragon!
For he snaps at alle that comes,
Snatching at his feast of Plums,
Snip! Snap! Dragon!

But Olde Christmasse makes hym come
Though he lookes so fee! fa! fum!
Snip! Snap! Dragon!

Don't 'ee feare him, bee but bold
Out he goes, his flames are colde,
Snip! Snap! Dragon!

Shakespearean Christmas Gifts

WITH QUOTES FROM *THE WINTER'S TALE* AND
THE SEVENTEENTH-CENTURY ACCOUNTS,
NICHOL'S PROGRESSES AND *ILLUSTRATIONS OF
MANNERS & EXPENCES*

It was customary to give New Year gifts in Elizabethan times, although it was not unknown to give one at Christmas itself. One wonders what sort of gifts the Bard would have most liked to receive. A new quill pen perhaps, or a knife to sharpen it, powder to blot his writing, and that scarce and expensive commodity, paper to write on. A pouch for his tobacco, an ounce of some fragrant new variety fresh and pungent, even hose or a ruff or a new cambric shirt would have been typical gifts to give a gentleman of his tastes and requirements.

In *The Winter's Tale* Autolycus, a rogue of a pedlar, comes in singing his wares thus:

> Lawn as white as driven snow;
> Cyprus black as e'er was crow;
> Gloves as sweet as damask-roses;

Masks for faces, and for noses;
Bugle-bracelet, necklace amber,
Perfume for a lady's chamber;
Golden quoifs and stomachers,
For my lads to give their dears;
Pins, and poking sticks of steel,
What maids lack from head to heel;
Come, buy of me, come; come buy, come buy;
Buy, lads, or else your lasses cry,
Come buy.

Clown: If I were not in love with Mopsa, thou shouldst take no money of me; but being enthralled as I am, it will also be to bindage of certain ribands and gloves.

Mopsa (a shepherdess): I was promised them against the feast; but they come not too late now.
[though the feast in this instance is the sheep-shearing feast in spring.]

According to William Sandys there was a distinct difference between New Year gifts and Christmas boxes.

The difference between New Year gifts and Christmas boxes appears to be that the former were mutually exchanged, or indeed were sometimes in the nature of an offering from an inferior to a superior, who made some acknowledgement in return, while the latter were in the nature of gratuities from superiors to their dependants. The practice is of considerable antiquity in this country, and formerly it was customary for the nobility and persons connected with the court to make presents to the king, who gave gifts, generally of money or plate in return ...

Sandys goes on to list 0at length gifts and costs of presents to various monarchs, the list of Queen Elizabeth I being of most interest to us here:

. . . Queen Elizabeth expected valuable ones [gifts]. They seem to have been much of the same description every year. The peers spiritual and temporal, ladies, gentlewomen, and officers of the household, etc. gave presents according to their rank and means, of money, rich dresses, jewels, etc.; the physicians and apothecary, boxes of ginger and candy; the cook and other domestics, or officers similar gifts to those hereafter mentioned.

These included such items as a pair of cloth of silver sleeves; collar & ruffs of gold damask embroidered with pearls; sugared fruits; a picture of the Holy Trinity; a fat goose and capon, a pair of oxen (from the cook!) and a box of ginger, nutmegs and sticks of cinnamon.

Mr Sandys' sources, *Nichol's Progresses* and *Illustrations of Manners & Expences*, give full accounts of the gifts received in the early years of Shakespeare's life, culminating with a gift from the Christmas Maskers in 1581 – too soon to have been one of Shakespeare's own troupe, though, as he would have been only about seventeen, still at home and not yet married. The gifts are interesting and help to show the reader the domestic spirit of the world in which Shakespeare lived. From it one may surmise that the Queen had a liking for candies and ginger, and that she received gifts from everyone – including her dustman! The list for the year 1577–8 shows:

Sir Gawen Carewe a smock of camerick, wrought with black silk in the collor and sleves, the square and ruffs wrought with Venice golde, and edged with a small bone lace of Venice gold. Also, by Phillip Sydney, a smock of camerick and a sute of ruffs cutworke with 4oz of spangles.

By Doctor Maister, a pot of grene gynger and other of orenge flowers.

By Smythsonne, Master Cooke, a feyer Marchpane.

By Dudley, Sergeant of the Pastry, a greate pye of Quynses and wardyns guilt. [A gilded pie of quince and plums.]

By Christofer Gyles, Cutler, a meate knyf with a feyer hafte of white bone and a conceyte in it.

By Morgan, Apotticary, thre boxes, one of gynger candy, another of grene gynger and the third orenge candit.

By Smyth, Dustman, two bolts of Camerick.

In 1578–9 the list included 'Morris Watkins, eighteen larkes in a cage.' Also mentioned were gowns, petticoats, kirtles, doublets, mantles, some embroidered with precious stones. Bracelets, jewels and ornaments. The list for 1581–2 is also interesting:

1581–2 Item a juell of golde, being a catt and myce playing with her, garnished with smale dyamondes and perle. Given by Lady Howarde.

Item, a flower of golde, garnished with sparcks of diamonds, rubyes, and ophales, with an agathe of her Majestis phisnamy, and a perle pendante, with devices painted in it. Geven by Eight Maskers in Christmas-weeke.

In 1589 she received a fan of red & white feathers, the handle gold and enamelled with a half moon of mother of pearl, within it sparks of diamonds and a few seed pearls on one side, and a picture of her within that. This came from Sir Francis Drake.

In return the queen gave money gifts, or gold or silver plate.

It was also the custom to send foodstuffs as presents and tenants might give a fat bird, or a cake as their means would allow, to their lord. Neighbours expecting an invitation to the party at the 'big house' would send anything from preserves, fruit, pies and cakes, eggs and cheeses, spices, meats and brawns. But from most of the records available, gifts were given, at this level anyway, with the hope of a return – money or gold from the monarch, an invitation from the local lord of the manor – or as a bribe, such as the gloves lined with 'angels' (money), given to Sir Thomas More when he was chancellor. It is reported that he graciously kept the gloves but returned the 'linings'. Sandys comments on this.

Formerly tenants used to make presents at this time to their landlords, frequently a capon, or something of similar value. The following is a list of food gifts sent to a landlord at Wootton by his tenants and neighbours:

Two sides of Venison, two half brawns, three pigs, ninety capons, five geese, six turkeys, four rabbits, eight partridges, two pullets, five sugar loaves, half a pound of nutmegs, one basket of apples and eggs, three baskets of apples, two baskets of pears.

Ceremonies
for Christmas

AN ACCOUNT IN VERSE OF THE CUSTOMS FOR
THE TWELVE DAYS OF CHRISTMAS

ROBERT HERRICK

Robert Herrick was born in the period when Shakespeare was beginning to gain acclaim as a playwright rather than as an actor. Born to a wealthy goldsmith's family in London, as a boy he would have been undoubtedly familiar with the name of the great Bard, if not his works. He moved back to his father's old county of Leicestershire to be apprenticed to his uncle, another goldsmith, who was knighted in 1605, and being accepted at court may well have attended some of the plays by Shakespeare put on for the Queen. Robert then went to Cambridge and eventually was ordained into the established English Church. Perhaps because of the resistance to folk culture by the Puritans, Robert developed a great interest in the old traditions of his early family days before his father died when, under Queen Elizabeth, Christmas retained its older customs and developed some new, elaborate ones too.

Hesperides was an outlet for his love of the old Christmas traditions and, together with his other seasonal verses, provides one of the most complete records of Christmas in Shakespearean England.

> Come guard this night the Christmas-pie,
> That the thief, though ne'er so sly,
> With his flesh-hooks, don't come nigh
> To catch it.
>
> From him, who all alone sits there,
> Having his eyes still in his ear,
> And a deal of nightly fear,
> To watch it.

The following was a warning to the maids that, according to superstition, a Christmas fire would not light unless all was clean, including the hands!

To Maids
Wash your hands or else the fire
Will not teend to your desire
Unwashed hands, ye maidens
know,
Dead the fire, though ye blow.

The Bell-man grew out of the Watchman, whose job was 365 days a year and not just for Christmas.

The Bell-Man
From noise of scare-fires rest ye free,
From murders, Benedicite!
From all mischances that may fright

Your pleasing slumbers in the night;
Mercy secure ye all, and keep
The goblins from ye, while ye sleep.
Past one o'clock, and almost two,
My Masters all, Good-day to you.

The following extract of a song, written to Sir Simon
Steward, tells the whole Christmas story.

CHRISTMAS SONG

... But here a jolly verse crowned with Ivy and
with Holly,
That tells of Winter's tales and mirth,
That milkmaids make about the hearth,
Of Christmas Sports, the Wassail Bowl,
That tost up, after fox-i-th'-hole;
Of Blind Man's Buff, and of the care
That young men have to shoe the Mare;
Of Twelve-tide cakes, of peas and beans,
Wherewith you make those merry scenes,
Whenas ye choose your king and queen,
And cry out, 'Hey for our town green';
Of Ash-heaps, in the which ye use
Husbands and wives by streaks to chose;
Of crackling Laurel, which foresounds
A plentious Harvest to your grounds:
Of these and suchlike things for shift,
We send in stead of New Year's Gift.
Read then, and when your face do shine,
With buxon meat and cap'ring wine,
Remember us, in cups full crowned,
and let our city health go round,
Quite through the young maids and the men

To the ninth number, if not ten.
Until the fired Chestnuts leap
For joy to see the fruits ye reap . . .

And let the russet swains the plough
And harrow hang up, resting now;
And to the bagpipe all address,
Till sleep takes place of weariness.
And thus, throughout, with Christmas plays
Frolic the full twelve holidays.

There were two types of wassail. That which one gave to
one's own crops and that which the wassailers visited upon
the household. The latter is described here.

THE WASSAIL

Give way, give way ye gates and win,
An easy blessing to your bin
And basket, by our entering in.

May both with Manchet stand replete;
Your larders too, so hung with meat,
That though a thousand, thousand eat.

Yet ere twelve moons shall whirl about
Their silv'ry spheres, that none may doubt
But more's sent in than was served out.
Next, may your dairies prosper so
As that your pans no ebb may know;
But if they do, the more to flow.

Like to a solemn sober stream
Bank'd all with lilies, and the cream

Of sweetest cowslips filling them.

Then may your plants be prest with fruit,
Nor bee or hive you have be mute;
But sweetly sounding like a lute.

Next, may your duck and teeming hen
Both to the Cock's tread say Amen;
And for their two eggs render ten.

Last, may your harrows, shears and ploughs,
Your stacks, your stocks, your sweetest mows,
All prosper by our virgin vows.

At New Year it was the traditional time to exchange gifts, rather than at Christmas itself. Herrick does not only tell us what customs were observed on this day, but presents them as his gift to the Court at Whitehall.

THE NEW-YEAR'S GIFT
Prepare for songs; He's come, he's come;
And let it be sin here to be dumb,
And not with lutes to fill the room.

Cast Holy-water all about,
And have a care no fire goes out,
But 'cense the porch and place throughout.

The altars all on fire be;
The storax fries, and ye may see
How heart and hand do all agree to make
things sweet.

Chorus: Yet all less sweet than He
Bring Him along, most pious priest,
And tell us then, whenas thou seest
His gently gliding, dove-like eyes,
How canst thou this Babe Circumcise?

Chorus: Back, back, again, each thing is done
With zeal alike, as twas begun;
Now singing, homeward let us carry
The Babe unto His mother Mary;
And when we have the Child commended
To the warm bosom, then our rites are ended.

On the eve of Epiphany the Star-boys visited, representing
the Wise Men following the star to the stable of Bethlehem.

STAR-SONG

1st traveller: Tell us, thou clear and heavenly
tongue,
Where is the Babe but lately sprung?
Lies he the Lily-banks among?

2nd traveller: Or say, if this new Birth of ours
Sleeps, laid within some ark of flowers,
Spangled with dew-light; thou canst clear
All doubts, and manifest the where.

3rd traveller: Declare to us, bright star, if we
seek
Him in the morning's blushing cheek,
Or search the beds of spices through,
To find him out.

Star: No, this ye need not do;
But only come and see him rest
A Princely Babe in's Mother's breast.

Chorus: He's seen! He's seen! why then a round,
Lets kiss the sweet and holy ground;
And all rejoice that we have found
A King before conception crown'd.
4th Traveller: Come then, come then, and let
us bring
Unto our pretty Twelfth-tide King,
Each one his several offering;

Chorus: And when the night comes, we'll give
Him wassailing;
And His treble honours may be seen,
We'll choose Him King and make His Mother,
Queen.

On Twelfth Day, the Feast of the Epiphany, religious
observances were made the evening before and then the
festivities began.

TWELFTH NIGHT OR KING & QUEEN
Now, now the mirth comes
With the cake full o' plums,
Where Bean's the king of Sport here;
Beside we must know, the pea also,
Must revel, as queen, in the court here.

Begin then to choose,
This night as ye use,
Who shall for the present, delight here,

Be a king by the lot, And who shall not
Be Twelfth-day queen for the night here.

Which known, let us make
Joy sops, with the cake;
And let not a man then be seen here,
Who unurg'd will not drink to the base from
the brink
A health to the queen and the king here.

Next crown the bowl full
With gentle lamb's wool:
Add sugar, nutmeg and ginger,
With a store of ale too, and thus ye must do
To make the wassail a swinger.

Give then to the king
And queen, wassailing:
And though with Ale ye be whet here,
Yet part ye from hence, as free from offence,
As when ye innocent met here.

Distaff's Day was the day after Twelfth Night, when the
women went back to their work (to their distaff or spinning). The men went on Plough Monday, which was the
first Monday after Twelfth Night, giving them, except
where Twelfth Night fell on a Sunday, a longer holiday
than the women!

St Distaff's Day

Partly work and partly play
Ye must on St Distaff's Day:
From the plough soon free your team,

Then come home and fodder them.
If the maids a spinning go,
Burn the flax and fire the tow;
Scorch their plackets, but beware
That ye singe no maidenhaire
Bring in pails of water then,
Let the maids bewash the men.
Give St Distaff all the right,
Then bid Christmas sport goodnight;
And next morrow, everyone,
To his own vocation.

The end of the Christmas season was 2 February, Candlemas, when all decorations must come down for fear of the spirits trapped in the evergreen boughs wreaking havoc.

CEREMONIES UPON CANDLEMAS EVE
Down with the Rosemary, and so
Down with the Bays and Mistletoe;
Down with the Holly, Ivy, all,
Wherewith ye drest the Christmas Hall:
That so the superstitious find
No one least branch left there behind:
For look, how many leaves there be
Neglected, there (maids, trust me)
So many goblins you shall see.

And finally for Candlemas Day:

Kindle the Christmas Brand, and then
Till sunset let it burn;
Which quench'd, then lay it up again

Till Christmas next return.
Part must be kept, wherewith to tend
The Christmas log next year,
And where 'tis safely kept, the fiend
Can do no mischief there.

Twelfth Day Feasts at Hampton Court

FROM THE DIARIES AND PAPERS OF
SIR DUDLEY CARLETON, 1604–7

In the early days of James I many Christmases were held at Hampton Court. Inigo Jones was by this time the favoured writer of the royal Christmas entertainment. His masques were elaborate, depending on expensive scenery and special effects, rather than on the excellence of wit and words of Shakespeare's plays, though many were full of topical jokes and innuendos. An important part of the festivities were the card games and at court the nobles, whom Elizabeth had tried hard to send home to their country estates for Christmas, played over vast sums of money getting themselves and their estates into often irrevocable debt, as can be seen from the following accounts.

Twelfth Day 1604

The Twelfth Day the French Ambassador was feasted publicly, and at night there was a play in the Queen's presence, with a masquerade of certain scotchmen; who came in with a sword dance, not unlike a matachin; and performed it cleanly; from whence the King went to dice, into his own presence, and lost 500 crowns which marred a gamester; for since he appeared not there but once before was it at in the same place and parted a winner. The Sunday following was the greete day of the Queene's masque, at which was present the Spanish and Polack ambassadors with their whole trains, and the most part of the Florentines and the Savoyards, but not the ambassadors themselves, who were in strong competition for place and precedence, that to displease neither it was thought best to let both alone.

January 8th 1607

On the Twelfth Eve there was a greate Golden play at Court. No Gamester admitted that brought not £300 at least. Montgomery played the King's money, and won him £750, which he had for his labour. The Lord Montegle lost the Queen £400, Sir Robert Cary, for the Prince, £300, and the Earl Salisbury, £300; the Lord Buckhurst, £500; *et sic coeteris*. So that I heard of no winner but the King and Sir Francis Wolley, who got about £800. The King went a Hawking-journey yesterday to Theobalds and returns tomorrow.

Above Westminster the Thames is quite frozen over; and the Archbishop came from Lambeth, on Twelfth-day, over the ice to Court. Many fanciful experiments are daily put in practice; as certain youths burnt a gallon of wine upon the ice, and made all the passengers partakers. But the best is, of an honest woman (they say) that had a great longing to encrease her family on the Thames!

John Chamberlaine, in a letter to Sir Dudley Carleton.

The Boar's Head Carol and The Christmas Prince

AN ACCOUNT OF AN ELIZABETHAN CUSTOM

WILLIAM SANDYS

Of the many known carols which refer to the noble meal, the following is the original one from the Elizabethan era. It was first sung before the Prince of Christmas at John the Baptist's College, Oxford during the festivities in 1607. A numerous court (of players) was appointed and the 'Prince', one Mr Thomas Tucker, with plays and pageants and entertainments continuing well past Christmas until Shrovetide.

It should be explained here that it was the custom throughout the land to elect a Prince for the season of Christmas, who would rule over the revels. His word was law. Christmas lasted much longer then than it does now, and frequently surpassed Twelfth Night and carried on until the feast of the Purification, Candlemas, on 2 February. Shrove Tuesday, what we now call Pancake Tuesday, was the end of feasting, for the next day began the long Lenten Fast of the Church in preparation for Easter.

An account from *The Christmas Prince*, reprinted by William Sandys in 1833, tells of the meal:

The first messe was a boar's head, which was carried in
by ye tallest and lustiest of all ye guard, before whom
(as attendants) wente first, one attired in a horesman's coat,
with a boars speare in his hande, next to him an other huntsman in greene, with a bloody faucion drawne; next to him
2 pages in tafatye sarcenet, each of yem with a messe of
mustard; next to whome came hee it carried ye boares-head
crost with a greene silke scarfe, by which hunge ye empty
scabbard of ye faulcion, which was carried before him. As
he entered ye hall, he sang this Christmas Caroll, ye three
last verses of euerie staffe being repeated after him by ye
whole companye.

> The Boar is dead,
> Lo, here is his head:
> What man could have done more
> Than his head off to strike,
> Meleanger like,
> And bring it as I do before?
>
> The living spoiled
> Where good men toiled,
> Which makes kind Ceres sorry;
> But now dead and drawn,
> Is very good brawn
> And we have brought it for ye.
>
> Then set down the swineyard,
> The foe to the vineyard,
> Let Bacchus crown his fall;
> Let this boar's head and mustard
> Stand for pig, goose and custard,
> And so you are welcome all.

Christmas at the Inns of Court

AN EXTRACT FROM *CUSTOMS AND CAROLS*

WILLIAM SANDYS

The custom of acting plays at court, at the City School of Westminster and at the Inns of Court was well established by Elizabeth's reign, and the year Shakespeare was born, the boys of Westminster School put on a performance called *Truth, Faithfulnesse & Mercye*. The Christmas Historian William Sandys takes up the story:

Masques and pageants were in great request as well as plays, and the Inns of Court vied with each other in the magnificence of their revels. In the 4th year of Elizabeth, there was a splendid Christmas kept at the Inner Temple, wherin Lord Dudley was the chief person, Constable & Marshall under the name Palaphilos, and Christopher Hatton (afterwards Chancellor) was Master of the Game. Previous to this, a sort of parliament was held on St Thomas' eve, to decide whether they should keep it, and if so, to publish the officers' names, and then, 'in token of joy and good liking, the bench and company pass beneath the hearth and sing a carol, and so to boyer.'

At these grand Christmases there were revels and dancing during the twelve days of Christmas. It was about this time that 'Ferrex and Porrex' was acted before the Queen by the gentlemen of the Inner Temple; the printer stating it to be 'for furniture of part of the grande Christmas in the Inner Temple.' The order of the usual Christmas amusements at the inns of Court of this period would cause some curious scenes if carried into effect in the present day. Barristers singing and dancing before the judges, serjeants, and benchers would 'draw a house' if spectators were admitted. Of so serious import was this dancing considered, that, by an order in Lincoln's Inn, of February 7th, James I under the barristers were by decimation put out of commons, because the whole bar offended by not dancing on Candlemas day preceding, according to the ancient order of the society, when the judges were present: with a threat that if the fault were repeated, they should be fined or disbarred. Dugdale gives the following description of the Inner Temple revels, the three grand days being All-Halloween, Candlemass, and Ascension Day.

First the solemn Revells (after dinner and the play ended) are begun by the whole House, Judges, Serjeants at Law, Benchers; the Utter and Inner Bar; and they led by the Master of Revells: and one of the Gentlemen of the Utter Barr are chosen to sing a song to the Judges, Serjeants or Masters of the Bench, which is usually performed; and in default thereof, there may be an amerciement. Then the Judges and the Benchers take their places, and sit down at the upper end of the Hall. Which done, the Utter-Barristers, and Inner-Barristers, perform a second solemn Revell before them. Which ended, the Utter-Barristers take their places and sit down. Some of the Gentlemen of the Inner-Barr, do present the House with dancing, which is called the Post-revells, and continue their Dances, till the Judges or Bench think meet to rise and depart.

In 1594 there was a celebrated Christmas at Grey's Inn, of which an account was published under the title of *Gesta Grayorum*, so called in consequence of the great popularity at that time of the *Gesta Romanorum*. The entertainments appear to have been heavy and pedantic in their nature, though suited to the style of the age. The concluding performance was a Masque before the Queen at Shrovetide containing much of that flattery which prevailed in all exhibitions before her. She was so much pleased with the performance, that on the courtiers dancing a measure after the Masque was ended, she exclaimed, 'What! Shall we have bread and cheese after a Banquet?' Mr Henry Helmes was the prince chosen, who assumed the following style, and had a numerous court to support him.

'The High and Mighty Prince Henry Prince of Purpoole, Arch-Duke of Stapulia de Bernardina, Duke of High and Nether Holborn, Marquis of St Giles and Tottenham, Court Palatine of Bloomsbury and Clerkenwell, Great Lord of the Cantons of Islington, Kentish-Town, Paddington and Knightsbridge, Knight of the most Heroical Order of the Helmet, and Sovereign of the same.'

These royal and public pageants lured many country gentlemen to the metropolis, who neglecting the comforts of their dependants in the country at this season, dissipated in town, part of their means for assisting them, and incapacitated themselves from continuing that hospitality for which the country had been so long noted. In order to check this practice, the gentlemen of Norfolk and Suffolk, were in 1589 commanded to depart for their countries, and there keep hospitality amongst their neighbours. The presence of the higher orders would have controlled the tendancy to drinking and riotous sports among the country people, which the resort of minstrels and other strollers at this time to taverns and ale-houses encouraged; while their real enjoyments would have been increased through the assistance and fostering care of their superiors.

Masques and plays with other Christmas festivities, continued throughout the reign of James I, and the Prince (Charles) himself occasionally performed and in particular gained great applause in Ben Jonson's Mask, *The Vision of Delight*, performed on Twelfth Night in 1617 when the Muscovy Ambassadors were entertained at Court.

On the Christmas Masque

A CRITIQUE OF BEN JONSON'S

MASQUE OF CHRISTMAS

LAURENCE WHISTLER

Laurence, brother of Rex, made a serious study of English festivals and produced a short dissertation on the masque, which was popular in Shakespeare's England. An extract from this account is reproduced here.

It was then (in the time of Henry VIII) that the name 'Masque' was given to a form of revel that would become, in time, the most beautiful ever contrived for an English Christmas.

Like the Orders of Architecture, the Masque came to us from Italy, and was grafted into a native tradition. There was no need to introduce fancy dress, dancing and pageantry to England: at King Henry's first Christmas the 'disguisings' had cost no less that £584. But the Court had taken no active part until 1513 . . . The Court ladies lost their shyness in time, and immensely enjoyed dressing up for the Masque. Though Queen Elizabeth did not care to take the floor herself . . .

With Ben Jonson to provide the words and Inigo Jones the machinery and costumes, the masques of the Stuart Court were in good hands – so long as the poet's taste and scholarship were dominant; for the poet kept all in proportion, verse, song, dance and architecture. To the greatest of English Architects the first three merely provided a grand excuse for the fourth.

The collaboration began with 'The Masque of Blackness' performed on Twelfth Night, 1605. In the old England, the festival was not an affair of one day, but of twelve – the Twelve Days of Christmas – and Shakespeare's *Twelfth Night* had been eminently a Christmas diversion, with a strong flavour of seasonable Misrule. Inigo Jones returned from Italy full of scenic splendours, but he attempted no extravagance at first . . .

Year after year poet and architect explored the possibilities of Masquing. Thus in Hue and Cry after Cupid Inigo Jones introduced the *scena ductilis*, in the form of a great red cliff rising between two richly trophied pillars . . . Thus again, at the royal wish, Ben Jonson introduced the Antimasque of the grotesque and clownish characters to act as foil (to the beautiful and splendid).

In Christmas, his Masque, such characters appear by themselves. It is a minor work quite outside the grand tradition, yet not without the genial charm, and for all its drowsy jokes it does give a lively impression of Father Christmas, the figure he cut in the 17th century, before anyone in England had ever heard of Santa Claus.

With The Tempus and Comus in mind, it seems ingenuous to add that good poets other than Ben Jonson were writing for the festivals and entertainments of the age. In the Lord's Masque of 1613 Thomas Campion made the stars dance on earth to celebrate the nuptials of Princess

Elizabeth. The last Masque before the Civil War was Inigo Jones' Salmacida Spolia – first under the brown fog of Calvinism. And yet, to believe that the Puritans really destroyed Christmas is like believing (and many do) that Dickens or the Prince Consort invented it!

Christmas lives! Loses one habit, acquires another, sometimes falls back into ancient ways – but lives.

The Masque of Christmas

BEN JONSON

Ben Jonson was playwright to Queen Elizabeth I and then James I. He and Shakespeare knew one another, and were often in the same location as they strove to please their majesties at court. In 1616, the year in which Shakespeare died, Jonson wrote and presented to the court of King James the most well known of all his works, **The Masque of Christmas**. An elaborate play, with costumes designed by Inigo Jones, this led the way for the great Twelfth Night costume balls which were enjoyed for the next three hundred years.

His characters each represented one of the elements of Christmas, personified. This being early post-Reformation days, one needed to be politically correct to survive. Thus references to 'Pope's-head-lane' refer to the old Roman Catholic religion which was not welcomed at court; also the reference to 'Friday-street' relates to the Catholic custom of the Friday fastday and abstinence from meat dishes. In order to be welcomed, Christmas is obviously anxious to show that, although his origins are in the old religion, he has moved with the times. The comic character of the old woman, Venus, exhibits the characteristics of the modern pantomime dame.

Directions
The Court being seated.
Enter CHRISTMAS *with two or three of the guard, attired in round Hose, long Stockings, a close Doublet, a high-crown'd Hat, with a Broach, a long thin beard, a Truncheon, little Ruffes, white Shoos, his Scarffes, and Garters tyed crosse, and his Drum beaten before him.*

Why, Gentlemen, doe you know what you doe? Ha! would you ha' kept me out? CHRISTMAS old Christmas, Christmas of London, and Capitayne Christmas? Pray you, let me be brought before my Ld. Chamberlayn. I'le not be answered else: Tis merry in hall when beards wag all: I ha' seen the time you ha' wish'd for me, for a merry Christmas; and now you ha' me, they would not let me in; I must come another time! a good jeast, as if I could come more than once a yeare; why I am no dangerous person, and so I told my friends o' the Guard. I am old Gregorie Christmas still, and though I come out of Pope's-head-alley, as good a protestant as any i' my Parish. The troth is, I ha' brought a Masque here, out o' the Citie, o' my own making, and doe present it by a sett of my Sonnes, that come out of the Lanes of London, good dancing Boyes all. It was intended, I confesse, for Curryers Hall; but because the weather has beene open, and the Livory not at leisure to see it till a Frost came, that they cannot worke, I thought it convenient, with some little Alterations, and the Groome o' the Revells hand to 't, to fit it for a higher Place; which I have done, and though I say it, another Manner of Device than your Newyeares night. Bones o' Bread, the King! (seeing his Mjty) Son Rowland! son Clem! be readie there in a trice: quick Boyes!

Enter his sons and daughters (ten in Number) led in, in a string, by CUPID who is attired in a flat capp, and a Prentice's coat, with Wings at his shoulders.

MISRULE in a Velvet Capp, with a sprigge, a short Cloke, great yellow ruffe (like a Reveller); his Torche-bearer bearing a Rope, a Cheese, and a Baskett.

CAROL, a long Tawny Coat, with a redd Capp, and a Flute at his Girdle; his Torche-bearer carrying a Song-booke open.

MINCED-PYE, like a fine Cook's wife, drest neat; her Man carrying a Pye, Dish and Spoones.

GAMBOL, like a Tumbler, with a Hoope and Bells; his Torche-bearer armed with a Colt-staff and a Binding-Cloth.

POST AND PAIR, with a Pair-royal of Aces in his Hat; his Garment all done over with Pairs and Purs; his Squire carrying a Boxe, Cards, and Counters.

NEW YEARE'S GIFT, in a blue coat, serving-man-like, with an Orange, and a Sprigge of Rosemary gilt on his head, his Hat full of Brooches, with a collar of Gingerbread; his Torche-bearer carrying a March-Pane with a Bottle of Wine on either arme.

MUMMING in a masquing pied suit, with a Vizard; her page bearing a browne Bowle, drest with Ribbands, and a Rosemary before her.

OFFERING, in a short Gowne, with a Porter's Staffe in his Hand, a Wyth borne before him, and a Bason, by his

Torche-bearer.

BABY-CAKE drest like a Boy, in a fine long Coat, Biggin-bib, Muck-ender, and a little Dagger; his Usher bearing a great Cake, with a Beane and Pease.

They enter singing.

Now God preserve, as you well doe deserve,
Your Majesties all two there;
Your Highnesse small, with my good Lords all,
And, Ladies, how doe you there?

Give me leave to ask, for I bring you a Masque
From little, little, little London,
Which saye the King likes, I have passed the Pikes,
If not, Old Christmas is undone.

(*Noise without*)

CHR. A' peace, what's the matter there?

GAMB. Here's one o'Friday-street would come in.

CHR. By no meanes, nor out of neither of the Fish-streets, admit not man; they are not Christmas creatures: Fish, and Fasting dayes, foe! Sonnes, say'd I well? looke to 't.

GAMB. No bodie out o' Friday-street, nor the two Fish-streets there; doe yo' heare?

CAROL. Shall John Butter o' Milke-street come in? aske him.

GAMB. Yes, he may slip in for a Torche-bearer, so he melt not too fast, that he wil; I last till the Masque be done.

CHR. Right, Sonne.

Sings agen

Our Dances freight, is a matter of eight,
and two, the which are Wenches;
In all they be ten, foure Cockes to a Hen,
and will swim to the tune like Tenches.
Each hath his Knight, for to carry his light,
Which some would say are torches;
To bring them here, and to lead them there,
and home again in their owne porches.
Now their intent –

Enter VENUS, a deafe Tire-woman

VEN. Now all the Lordes blesse me, where am I, tro? where is Cupid? Serve the King? they may serve the Cobler well enough, some of 'em, for any courtesie they have, y'wisse; they ha' need o' mending; unrude people they are, your Courtiers, here was thrust upon thrust indeed! was it ever so hard to get in before, tro?

CHR. How now? what's the matter?

VEN. A place, forsooth, I do want a place; I would have a good place to see my Child act in before the King, and the Queenes Majesties (God blesse 'em) to night.

CHR. Why, here is no place for you.

VEN. Right forsooth, I am Cupid's Mother, Cupid's own Mother, forsooth; yes forsooth; I dwell in Pudding-lane; ay, forsooth, he is Prentise in Lovelane with a Bugle-maker,* that makes your Bobs, and Bird-bolts for Ladies.

CHR. Good Lady Venus of Pudding-lane, you must go out for all this.

VEN. Yes, forsooth, I can sit any where, so I may see my Cupid act; hee is a pretty Child, though I say it that perhaps should not, you will say; I had him by my first Husband. He was a Smith forsooth, we dwelt in Doelittle-lane then, he came a moneth before his time, and that may make him somewhat imperfect; but I was a Fishmonger's daughter.

CHR. No matter for your Pedigree, your house; good Venus, will you depart?

VEN. Ay, forsooth, he'le say his part, I warrent him, as well as ere a Play boy of 'em all; I could ha' had money enough for him, an I would ha' been tempted, and ha' let him out by the weeke, to the King's Players; Master Burbadge has been about and about with me; and so has old Mr. Hemings too, they ha' need of him, where is he tro'a? I would faine see him, pray God they have given him some drinke since he came.

CHR. Are you ready Boyes? strike up, nothing will drown this noisesome dame but a Drum: a' peace, yet, I ha' not done. SING –
Now, their intent is about to present –

CAROL. Why, here be halfe of the properties forgotten, Father.

OFFERING. Post and Pair wants his pur-chops and his pur-dogs.

CAROL. Ha' you nere a Son at the Groom-Porters to beg or borrow a paire of Cards quickly?

GAMB. It shall not need, heer's your Son Cheater without, has Cards in his pocket.

OFFERING. Odds so; speake to the Guard to let him in, under the name of a propertie.

GAMB. And heer's New-yeare's-gift ha's an Orenge, and Rosemarie, but not a clove to stick in't.

NEW-YEAR. Why let one go to the Spicery.
CHR. Fie, fie, fie; 'tis naught, it's naught, boyes.

VEN. Why, I have Cloves, it be cloves you want, I have cloves in my purse, I never go without one in my mouth.

CAROL. And Mumming has not his Vizard neither.

CHR. No matter, his owne face shall serve for a punishment, and 'tis bad enough; has Wassell her boule, and Minc'd-pie her spoones?

OFFERING. I, I; but Mis-rule doth not like his suite: he saies they Players have lent him one too little, on purpose, to disgrace him.

CHR. Let him hold his peace, and his disgrace will bee the lesse: what? shall wee proclaime where wee were furnisht?

Mum! Mum! a' peace, be readie, good Boyes.

Sings agen

Now their intent, is above to present,
With all the appurtainements
A right Christmas, as, of old, it was,
To be gathered out of the dances.

Which they do bring, and afore the king,
The Queen, and Prince, as it were now,
Drawn here by love; who over and above,
Doth draw himself in the geer too.

(*Here the drum and fife sounds and they march about once. In
the second coming up,* CHRISTMAS *proceeds to his Song.*)

Hum, drum, sauce for a coney;
No more of your martial music;
Even for the sake O' the next new stake
For there I do mean to use it.

And now to ye, who in place are to see
With roll and farthingale hoopèd,
I pray you know, though he want of his bow,
By the wings, that this is CUPID.

He might go back, for to cry 'What you lack?'
But that were not so witty:
His cap and coat are enough to note
That he is the Love o' the City.

And he leads on, though he now begone,

For that was his only rule:
But now comes in Tom of Bosoms-Inn,
And he present-eth MISRULE.

Which you may know, by the very show,
Albeit you never ask it:
For there you may see what his ensigns be,
The rope, the cheese and the basket.

This CAROL plays, and has been in his days
A chirping boy, and a kill-pot.
Kit cobler it is, I'm a father of his,
And he dwells in the lane called Fill-pot.

But how is this? O my daughter Cis,
MINCED-PIE, with her do not dally
On pain o' your life; she's an honest cook's wife,
And comes out of Scalding-Alley.

Next in the trace, comes GAMBOL in place,
And to make my tale the shorter,
My son, Hercules, tane out of Distaff Lane,
But an active man, and a porter.

Now POST & PAIR, old Christmas's heir,
Doth make and a gingling sally;
And wot you who, tis one of my two
Sons, card-makers in Purr-alley.
Next, in a trice, with his box and his dice
Mac' pipin my son, but younger,
Brings MUMMING in; and the knave will win,
For he is a coster-monger.

But NEW-YEAR'S GIFT, of himself makes shift
To tell you what his name is;
With orange on head, and his gingerbread,
Clem Waspe, of Honey lane 'tis.

This, I tell you, is our jolly WASSEL,
And for Twelfth Night more meet too;
She works by the ell, and her name is Nell,
And she dwells in Threadneedle Street too.

Then OFFERING, he, with his dish and his tree,
That in every great house keepeth,
Is by my son, young Littleworth, done,
And in Penny-Rich Street sleepeth.

Last BABY-CAKE, that an end doth make
Of Christmas merry, Christmas vein-a,
Is child Rowlan, and a straight young man,
Though he comes out of crooked Lane-a.

There should have been, and a dozen, I ween,
But I could find but one more
Child of Christmas, and a LOG it was,
When I had them all gone o'er.

I prayed him, in a tune so trim,
That he would make one to prance it:
And I myself, would have been the Twelfth,
O! but LOG was too heavy to dance it.

Now Cupid, come you on.
CUPID. You worthie wights, King, Lordes and Knights,
O Queen, and Ladies bright:

Cupid invites you to the sights
He shall present to night.

VEN. 'Tis a good child, speake out, hold up your head, love.

CUPID. And which Cupid ... And which Cupid ...

VEN. Do not shake so Robin, if thou beest a-cold, I ha' some warme waters for thee here.

CHR. Come, you put Robin Cupid out, with your waters, and your fisling; will you be gone?

VEN. I forsooth, he's a child, you must conceive, and must be us'd tenderly; he was never in such an assembly before, forsooth, but once at the Warmoll Quest, forsooth, where he said grace as prettily as any of the Sheriffes Hinchboyes, forsooth.

CHR. WILL YOU PEACE, FORSOOTH?

VEN. I, that's a good boy, speake plaine, Robin; how does his Majestie like him, I pray? will he give him eight pence a day thinke you? Speake out Robin.

CHR. Nay, he is out enough, you may take him away, and begin your Dance; this is to have speeches.

VEN. You wrong the Child, you doe wrong the Infant, I 'peale to his Majestie.

Here they dance.

CHR. Well done, Boyes, my fine Boyes, my Bully Boyes.

Sings agen
THE EPILOGUE

Nor doe you think their legges is all
the commendation of my Sons,
For at the Artillery-Garden they shall
as well (forsooth), use their Guns.

And march as fine, as the Muses nine,
along the streets of London:
And i' their brave tires, to gi' their false fires,
especially Tom, my Son.

Now if the lanes and the alleys afford
such an activity as this;
At Christmas next, if they keep their word
can the Children of Cheapside miss?

Tho', put the case, when they come in place,
they should not dance, but hop;
Their very gold lace, with their silk would 'em grace,
having so many knights o' the shop.

But were I so wise, I might seem to advise
so greate a potentate as yourselfe;
They should, sir, I tell 'e, spar't out of their belly
and this way spend some of their pelf.

Ay, and come to the Court, for to make you some Sport,
at leaste once every yeare:

As Christmas hath done, with his seventh or eighth Son,
and his couple of Daughters deare.

THE END

Many of the quips and references here are topical, the
addresses local and, no doubt, some of the references have
a double meaning and a bawdy intent. The whole introduc-
tion would be interspersed with much laughter from the
audience, as the 'children' pranced and mimed to the rhym-
ing introductions from their 'father', Christmas, who tried
hard to get his acts together literally while Venus continued
her devastating interruptions. From this play it may be seen
that the early Jacobean audience, such as Shakespeare was
writing for, would have been as much at home with the
frivolous pantomime season as we are today.

'A Christmas Carroll'

THE CHRISTMAS SEASON IN VERSE

GEORGE WITHER

George Wither was a poet born in Hampshire in 1588. The son of a country gentleman, he went to Oxford to study the classics until family financial problems, brought about by the fines paid to the Crown by all recusant Catholics at that time, meant that George had to go home and tend the plough. This task did not suit him and he quickly escaped to London where he sought to make his fortune at the royal court.

Disenchanted with court life, he was sent to prison for writing satirical poems about the life there and while in prison wrote some of his best pieces including **Juvenilia**, from which the following poem comes. It describes vividly the Christmas experienced in the late sixteenth century, although some of the references are not immediately obvious. Verse 5 tells us that the poor man who pawns his rings and clothing all year retrieves them for Christmas, while the barmaid has been saving up by scraping the dregs from the beer barrels to sell for her own pennies. Verse 7 strikes at the matter close to Queen Elizabeth's heart, that of the landlords staying in London instead of going home to their estates and looking after their tenants. This task fell to the home farmers, who kept up the tradition of giving the workers and farm labourers a joint of meat, and a pie or cake. Verse 10 speaks of many old customs – the 'wenches with their wassail bowls' are of course the Vessel maidens from ancient times, who survived into living memory in parts of Britain. The 'Wild Mare' is another remnant of pagan belief, carried on in the Welsh 'Mari Lwyd,' and the kitchen boy's broken box is the clay money box which servants made to collect their Christmas gift from their employers, hence 'Christmas Box' meaning a gift and 'Boxing Day' meaning the day when servants went around to collect their money. Verse 11 refers to the customs of Twelfth Night, when a King and Queen were chosen to rule the revels and master and servant changed places, sometimes called the 'Topsy-Turvy' feast.

1

So, now is come our joyful'st feast;
Let every man be jolly.
Each room with Ivy-leaves is dress'd
And every post with holly.
Though some churls at our mirth repine,
Round your foreheads garlands twine,
Drown a sorrow in a cup of wine,
And let us all be merry.

2

Now all our neighbour's chimneys smoke,
And Christmas blocks are burning;
Their ovens they with baked meats choke,

And all their spits are turning.
Without the door let sorrow lie,
And if for cold it hap to die,
We'll bury't in a Christmas Pie,
And evermore be merry.

3

Now every lad is wondrous trim,
And no man minds his labour;
Our lasses have provided them
A bagpipe and a tabour.
Young men, and maids, and girls and boys,
Give life to one another's joys,
And you anon shall by their noise
Perceive that they are merry.

4

Rank misers now do sparing shun,
Their hall of music soundeth;
And dogs thence with whole shoulders run,
So all things there aboundeth.
The country folk themselves advance,
For crowdy-mutton's come out of France;
And Jack shall pipe, and Jill shall dance,
And all the town be merry.

5

Ned Swash hath fetched his bands from pawn,
And all his best apparel;
Brisk Nell hath bought a Ruff of Lawn
With droppings of the Barrel;
And those that hardly all the year
Had bread to eat or rags to wear,

Will have both clothes and dainty fare,
And all the days be merry.

6

Now poor men to the Justices
With Capons make their arants,
And if they hap to fail of these
They plague them with their warrants.
But now they feed them with good cheer,
And what they want they take in beer,
For Christmas comes but once a year,
And then they shall be merry.

7

Good farmers in the country nurse
The poor, that else were undone.
Some landlords spend their money worse,
On lust and pride at London.
There the roysters they do play,
Drab and dice their land away,
Which may be ours another day;
And therefore let's be merry.

8

The client now his suit forbears,
The prisoner's heart is eased,
The debtor drinks away his cares,
And for the time is pleased.
Though others' purses be more fat,
Why should we pine or grieve for that?
Hang sorrow, care will kill a cat,
And therefore let's be merry.

9

Hark, how the wags abroad do call
Each other forth to rambling;
Anon you'll see them in the Hall,
For nuts and apples scrambling.
Hark, how the roofs with laughters sound!
Anon they'll think the house goes round,
For they the cellar's depth have found,
And there they will be merry.

10

The wenches with their Wassail bowls,
About the streets are singing,
The boys are come to catch the Owls,
The Wild Mare in is bringing.
Our kitchen boy hath broke his box,
And to the dealing of the Ox
The honest neighbours come by flocks
And here they will be merry.

11

Now Kings and Queens poor sheep-cotes have.
And mate with everybody;
The honest now may play the knave,
The wise men play at noddy.
Some youths will now a-mumming go,
Some others play at Rowland-Hoe,
And twenty other gameboys moe,
Because they will be merry.

12

Then wherefore in these merry days
Should we, I pray, be duller?

No; let us sing some roundelays
To make our mirth the fuller.
And, whilst thus inspir'd we sing,
Let all the streets with echoes ring;
Woods, and hills, and everything,
Bear witness we are merry.

'To Shorten Winter's Sadness'

FROM THOMAS WEELKES' MADRIGALS

To shorten winter's sadness
See where the nymphs with gladness
Disguised are all a-coming,
Right wantonly a-mumming.
    Fa-la

Whilst youthful sports are lasting,
To feasting turn our fasting;
With revels and with Wassails
Make grief and care our vassals.
    Fa-la

For youth it will beseemeth
That pleasure he esteemeth;
And sullen age is hated
That mirth would have abated.
    Fa-la

Acknowledgements

The comments and eccentricities of some of the critics quoted in this book are not necessarily in accord with my own thoughts. The original grammar and spelling has been retained in most extracts and for this reason there may be inconsistencies. *The Masque of Christmas* by Ben Jonson is pieced together from two copies, *The Book of Christmas & New Yeare* (1860) and *Righte Merrie Christmasse* (1890). References are also made to the following: *Ben Jonson*, Herford and Percy (Oxford, 1925), *The Masque of Christmas*, Whistler which uses the Carisbrook Library version of 1890, 'Dissitation on the Masques', Whistler from The Masque of Christmas. 'Now Thrice Welcome Christmas' by George Wither is taken from *Poor Robins Kalendar*. The quote on a seventeenth-century Christmas dinner was taken from *The English Housewife* by Gervase Markham. Research for 'Shakespearean Christmas Presents' included details from the following sources: W. Sandys, *Carols Old and New* (1833); Nichols' *Progresses and Illustrations of Manners & Expences* (1647); W. Sandys, *Christmastide* (1830) and numerous others. The extract from Christmas at the Mermaid comes from Theodore Watts-Dunton's book, *Christmas at the Mermaid* (John Lane, 1902).

All other research and editing were taken from a variety of sources in the original Christmas Archives collection now in the custodianship of the Felissimo Corporation of Kobe Japan.

Edited and updated by Andrew Hubert von Staufer.

You may also enjoy ...